PROPHET PRIEST & KING

A Novel

Cornell Graham

Cover photo by Cornell Graham
Book design by Cornell Graham

ISBN: 0-9715949-0-2
First printing - February 2002

For additional copies of this book , feedback or other inquiries,
please address to:

Cornell Graham
P.O. Box 2124
Alpharetta, GA 30023

Printed in the United States by
Morris Publishing
3212 East Highway 30
Kearney, NE 68847
1-800-650-7888

I proudly dedicate this debut novel to
my brother

OMEGA GRAHAM, JR.
August 29, 1962 – December 10, 1987

ACKNOWLEDGEMENTS

Thank you dear Father for your love, wisdom, mercy and grace. Indeed, you are the reason for my being. All that I have is from your loving hand. You're the only Father that I've ever really known, and I now know that you're the only one that I'll ever really need. Despite my shortcomings you continue to lift me up – for this I am eternally grateful. All praise and glory to you, my dear Father – both now and forever more.

Thanks to my wife, Debra; my son, Zachary; and my daughter, Kristyna for your loving support and patience during the time I've had to spend writing this book.

And to all of you who were kind enough to read a portion of the manuscript or the entire contents – from its initial version to its revised version – I say thank you! I won't mention names lest I fail to include someone, but you guys know who you are.

Finally, I thank in advance the many readers of this book. I appreciate your support and truly hope that you will find this book an enjoyable read.

CHAPTER ONE

EVERY NOW AND THEN THE DAUNTING questions emanated from within the corridors of his brain and knocked relentlessly, like an unwanted solicitor. Was it really a simple case of insomnia? Or was it his overwhelming ambition that continuously sought to rob him mercilessly of the minimum requisite eight hours of sleep of each night? His continual loss of sleep over the past ten years bothered him greatly. Especially since Harvard Prophet was not accustomed to losing anything.

Although his sixty-three year-old, six-foot tall masculine frame had learned to adapt to receiving only four or five hours of nightly shut-eye, he vehemently resented the seemingly uncontrollable depravation. Last night, however, he fought back against the ethereal forces holding his body hostage and victoriously reclaimed what he believed to be a very important part of his well being.

Despite the vigorous onslaught of thunderstorms throughout the Atlanta area last night, Harvard Prophet had experienced one of the most *peaceful* nights for sleeping that he could remember in quite some time. As he slept, he had been oblivious to the raging storm that battled outside his Italian, Renaissance-styled mansion. Only the *Civil War* had ever left such a devastating path of destruction. Driving rains, accompanied by boisterous thunder, had roared through the southern city like a freight train out of control. Pine trees snapped like toothpicks as gusty winds exhaled their forceful breath. Power lines bowed in deftly submission, while lightning flickered repeatedly across the nighttime sky, like a flash from a cheap camera gone haywire. Yet, Harvard had managed to achieve a delightful respite.

As head of the hottest advertising agency in the country, he'd confronted his fair share of storms. His agency, Prophet, Priest & King, or PPK, as it was sometimes referred to, has successfully survived every conceivable storm that had mounted an attack against it. Harvard had come to realize over the years that such havoc came with the territory. The rapid creation of a $100 million advertising agency was inevitably bound to attract storm fronts of various proportions, he rationalized.

This particular Monday marked the tenth anniversary for PPK as a full-service advertising agency. It was going to be a momentous occasion. There were accolades to be properly dispersed not just within the closely guarded PPK agency, but amongst their loyal clientele as well. In fact, ever since Harvard Prophet formed PPK, the renowned ad agency has never lost a client. It was an impressive footnote. He knew it. Their clients knew it. His competitors knew it. And it was a feat that Harvard had no intentions of allowing anyone to change.

Absolutely no one.

After last night's inquietude, the air on this early morning in June was now cool and crisp. Harvard slowly extended his right hand upward and used his thumb to depress the button on the ceiling inside his neatly polished black Jaguar sedan, and then he watched nonchalantly as the sunroof slid backwards. Immediately he felt a rush of coolness infiltrate the silver gray hairs of his head. He gave a quick glance into the rearview mirror to make certain that his hair, which was beginning to thin on the sides, was still neatly groomed and in place. He was quite meticulous about his appearance. And while the wrinkles that lined his leathery complexion were as visible as those on an un-ironed shirt, he considered himself to be a very handsome man.

The drive to PPK's offices from Harvard's Buckhead mansion was no more than ten minutes if he left by 6:30, which he promptly did on this Monday morning.

The Buckhead area of Atlanta was considered by some to be the *crème de la crème* of communities. It was an upscale area reluctantly bordered within the Atlanta city limits, and where the streets were littered with multi-million dollar homes and the driveways served as valet attendants to Range Rovers and

Mercedes-Benzes. And although some ofAtlanta's young professional athletes and pop stars maintained high-rise residences in the Buckhead area, Harvard believed that it was definitely an old-money type community. The kind of money that never seemed to run out - it just changed hands from generation to generation.

Harvard Prophet, however, wasn't privy to such aristocracy. He was neither born into such a societal caste nor was he blessed with any wealthy and refined family connections. Nevertheless, he now believed that he belonged among Atlanta's privileged few. And while it was the prevailing thought, at least among those who'd inherited such rich status and class, that one could not *buy* his way into the upper echelon of society, Harvard had determined rather early on in his life that *everything* had its price.

Everything and everybody.

As the sleek Jaguar rolled quietly and seemingly effortlessly along Peachtree Street toward downtown Atlanta, Harvard chose to ignore the overweight sport utility vehicle that had been riding on his bumper for the past several blocks. He was in much too good of a mood to be rattled this morning. Undeniably, rush-hour traffic in Atlanta had become an enigma to him. He could never quite figure out why it was even referred to as rush hour when drivers were lucky if their speedometers could reach *twenty-five miles* per hour in the daily snarling congestion.

As the ever-increasing and impatient traffic converged toward the heart of the city, Harvard reflected with buoyancy on the past ten years of events that culminated his current success.

Harvard Prophet had always wanted to run his own advertising agency, though he never worked for one prior to buying what was then *Priest & King* – a relatively small outfit billing only $5 million per year. Two men, who had earlier defected from the Chicago branch of the New York powerhouse ad agency *J. Walter Baxter,* headed the tiny agency. Duke Priest was then twenty-nine, and his partner Princeton King, was twenty-seven. Both men had been hired as copywriters at JWB.

When Duke and Princeton left Chicago to start their own agency in Atlanta, both had big dreams of making their newly formed shop a serious contender among Atlanta's growing advertising agency titans. However, Priest & King peaked at $5 million in billings before things began a downward spiral.

The year was 1990 when Harvard Prophet approached Priest & King about a buy-out. One year had passed since he'd buried his wife, Diana. He was on sabbatical from his position as director of advertising for the *Atlanta Post-Gazette,* the southeast's largest daily newspaper. When he'd taken the sabbatical after Diana's death, he knew then that he would never return to the newspaper business. After having spent his entire career with one organization - thirty years to be exact - Harvard had developed an ardent desire to run his own ad agency.

Not surprising to him, his offer to purchase Priest & King was politely rejected by both partners. Of course, Harvard refused to take *no* for an answer. He spared little expense as he wined and dined the young cohorts at some of Atlanta's most lavish restaurants. But the two partners still would not accept his offer. Their reasoning was simple. They'd come to enjoy the freedom that owning their small shop had afforded them. They hadn't become millionaires, but neither Duke nor Princeton had entered the business for the money. And despite their lack of financial prowess, both men knew that their agency was a viable part of their lives. For them it was an outlet for their creative expression.

However, some three weeks after his initial offer was made, Harvard Prophet was hand-delivering a cashier's check payable to Duke Priest and Princeton King. Harvard had successfully acquired a seventy-percent controlling interest in the small agency, leaving each partner with a fifteen-percent share. He'd bargained hard for the full one hundred percent, yet decided to settle for the seventy with a strong determination to get the other thirty-percent one way or another.

It was never quite understood by Duke and Princeton why Harvard was so obsessed with buying their little, relatively unknown, agency. It was obvious that the man could have chosen from a litany of other well-known shops or simply started his own. Later, however, they would learn that the old man had a fixation for their airline account, which billed only $2 million a year.

Harvard Prophet considered himself fortunate to have even been in a financial position to pursue his life-long quest. His wife's demise left him with a large sum of money – money that she'd inherited a few years earlier from her parent's abundant wealth. He would have preferred to realize his dream using his own capital resources, but that would have been nearly impossible since his salary at the Atlanta Post-Gazette only garnered him $60,000 per year. His wife, on the other hand, not only had access to a substantial inheritance, but she also made almost three-times his salary as a senior vice president for *The Coca-Cola Company*.

Harvard nearly lost all hope of ever owning an ad agency until one Saturday afternoon, a year before Diana's death, he happened across a large manila envelope lying atop the cluttered papers on his wife's desk in their home study. The envelope's return address listed the name of an Atlanta prominent law firm. It was addressed solely to Mrs. Diana Prophet, and printed just below the red postage-meter stamp, in large block letters, were the words PERSONAL & CONFIDENTIAL. Harvard picked up the envelope and observed that it had already been opened. Without hesitation he simply removed the contents. Inside the envelope was a *Will* that Diana apparently had prepared. She'd name him as sole beneficiary of everything she owned - the inheritance and a $500,000 life insurance policy, which he wasn't aware even existed. The Will had also given specific instructions that in the event of her untimely death, Harvard was to establish a trust fund on behalf of their daughter Hannah, then eleven years of age. His immediate thoughts after reading the Will was that his wife had been diagnosed with an incurable illness - cancer had run in her family.

In the days, weeks and months that followed the discovery of his wife's last Will and Testament; Harvard had waited for Diana to break the painful news to him.

The news never came.

Harvard even tried dropping subtle hints to her in an effort to coax his wife into discussing the Will and whatever traumatic event awaited her. But Diana was either oblivious to his subtlety or determined to keep her news private. She seemed and behaved as any normal forty-two year-old corporate executive, wife and mother would.

Seven months later, however, Harvard was awakened by a late night telephone call from the Tennessee State Highway Patrol. Diana's black Mercedes SL had been found crushed and burned at the bottom of an embankment along Interstate 24 near Chattanooga. Diana's body had been burned beyond recognition. Her dental records would later identify her remains.

She'd been returning to Atlanta from a public relations seminar in Nashville. His wife hated to fly – choosing instead to drive herself to out-of-town meetings whenever possible. It would prove to be one of the few wrong choices made during her lifetime. Police reports would later conclude that Diana Prophet had apparently fallen asleep at the wheel.

Harvard gently dabbed the corners of his rheumy eyes with the tip of his long, pointy index finger as he recalled the difficulty that he had experienced in telling his young daughter that her mother was dead. The ensuing weeks and months proved to be an arduous time period. Suddenly, he'd become a fifty-two year-old father with an eleven year-old daughter to nurture and raise alone. Of course, Hannah had the benefit of a live-in Nanny who'd been with the family since their daughter's birth.

Harvard was grateful for the money. It certainly came in handy at just the right time in his life. What he could never quite figure out, however, was why Diana chose to keep her riches a secret. The inheritance totaled just over $2.7 million. Had he known sooner just how much his wife had, he would have left the Atlanta Post-Gazette years earlier. But Diana never gave the slightest indication of her small millions. She'd been content living in their modestly furnished two-story brick home in a North Atlanta suburb.

Harvard nodded his head incredulously. He now realized that they could have lived in a home at least five-times the size of the one Diana was content to reside. Money and status did not easily impress the woman. Even the Mercedes she drove had been a gift from her parents after she was promoted to a senior vice president.

Diana's father had been her consummate champion. He'd made most of his fortune buying Coca-Cola stock. He was always praising the company at every opportunity - raving about how Coca-Cola is the cornerstone of Atlanta's building block of success. So naturally, when his daughter had joined the big soft drink maker right out of college, Diana's father was beside himself, to say the least.

Harvard had tried to maintain a respectable relationship with Diana's parents at best. He'd always suspected, however, that it was her father who dominated and influenced his wife's financial affairs, and with no regards to him as her husband. He figured that her father must have believed that if his daughter revealed to her husband her impending inheritance it might have had detrimental effects on their marriage.

Upon that thought, Harvard couldn't contain the sheepish grin that slowly formed across his face as he whipped the Jaguar into the *reserved* space of the parking garage at PPK's office tower. Perhaps the old son-of-a-gun had been right all along, he whispered silently. Money *did* a have way of making people do detrimental things.

CHAPTER TWO

WITH JUST OVER ONE HUNDRED employees, *Prophet, Priest & King* occupy the entire seventeenth floor of the Peachtree Towers building in downtown Atlanta. His Piaget Swiss watch displayed ten minutes before seven as Harvard strode from the elevators. He had adopted his own style of walking. And since he considered himself to be a unique man, in every sense of the word, he wanted everything about him to reflect his paragon style.

The pace of his steps this morning were slower than usual as he made his way down the dimly-lit corridor toward his spacious corner office suite. The way in which he lifted his left leg slightly as he walked made him appear cool and hip. This old white man had arrived.

Harvard Prophet's bullish eyes surveyed the immaculate surroundings as he admired the agency's posh facilities. The large PPK corporate logo, sculptured in bronze letters, greeted anyone stepping off the elevators directly into the reception area, which was expansive. The receptionist's center was constructed of cherry wood veneers. A *Baccarat* vase housed an assortment of fresh cut flowers daily as it sat prominently atop the receptionist's counter, displaying its splendid array of colorful beauty.

Harvard insisted that the office environment project a contemporary image as well as an image of unquestionable success. It was by his design and desire that senior management occupy enclosed offices. He refused to follow the prevailing corporate trend of *open offices* for his comrades. He reasoned that when one reached a certain level of management, one's privacy at the office became not just consequential, but imminently important, and vitally necessary.

The remaining employees or *support people,* as Harvard referred to them, performed their tasks at customized workstations. The workstations had a surface area that was spacious enough to maintain a PC, scanner, printer and fax machine - all the necessary tools of today's corporate trade.

Harvard unlocked the large mahogany door to his office. He used the same key that he used to unlock his office door to flip on the light switch. The recessed lights in the ceiling flickered momentarily before the enormous room sprung to life. His office suite was an impressive eighteen by thirty feet. The massive mahogany desk, which had been imported from France, was huge enough to seat at least eight people around it in a conference-table-style fashion.

He trotted over to his matching credenza and quickly dropped his genuine leather attaché case on top of it. He noticed that he'd received a letter on his private fax machine that was positioned at the other end of the credenza. He gave little thought to the letter's content as he walked over to retrieve it.

CorpAir, Inc. last evening had sent the fax. CorpAir was PPK's largest client, representing one-half of the agency's $100 million in annual billings. The fax consisted of just one page – a neatly typed and well-articulated letter addressed to Mr. Harvard Prophet, President and Chief Creative Officer.

Noticeably impatient, he removed the *Ben Franklin* reading glasses from the breast pocket of his tailored suit jacket and placed them just slightly on his nose. The metal frame was cold as it came to rest against his aging skin. It appeared as though he was looking over the top of the spectacles instead of through them. He began reading the letter. Despite its conformity to proper business etiquette, the letter was short and to the point.

"Well, I'll be damned!" he shouted aloud, after finishing the letter. He cursed some more and banged his tightly coiled fist against his desk, rattling some paper clips that were resting comfortably in a brass cup that sat atop his desk. He slowly moved over to a wall of windows that stretched from the ceiling to the floor. He was fuming inside as he stared at the crawling traffic below. From his vantage point, the cars looked like an army of ladybugs scurrying for food. He read the disturbing letter again, focusing more closely on every word. He began shaking his head in disgust.

CorpAir had announced their intention to place their advertising account up for *review*. It essentially meant that his huge and profitable client was interested in a new ad agency. Traditional protocol dictated that CorpAir comprise an enviable list of advertising agencies and invite them to make formal presentations to their senior management. The competing agencies would all pursue the account vigorously in an attempt to score a victory for the coveted CorpAir brand.

More than likely, the presentations would spare no expense as those agencies fortunate enough to be granted an opportunity to showcase their creative capabilities and their management competency would spend whatever was necessary with high hopes of adding another $50 million to their already bulging annual billings. Of course, PPK would also be invited to participate in the review. It was a *courtesy* the client usually afforded the incumbent agency.

Someone named *Christine Armstrong* had sent the letter. Harvard recognized the name as that of CorpAir's new vice president of marketing. This is unbelievable, he thought to himself. The woman had just been appointed the vice-presidency last week! She sure as hell didn't waste any time throwing her authority around!

Harvard cursed himself for failing to meet with her last week. He realized that it didn't take much to tick off a client. His anger intensified. Partly because he maintained a close and cordial relationship with

CorpAir's CEO, Douglas Sheldon. Why didn't Douglas send the letter? Or, better yet, why couldn't Douglas have called him directly to discuss this impending move? But to have some prissy VP send the bad news - over a lousy fax - was so unlike Douglas Sheldon. And Harvard made a mental note to tell him so at the very next opportunity.

"Dammit!" he shouted even louder this time, tossing the letter towards his desk and then watching it glide to the plush carpeted floor. He couldn't let them do this to him! CorpAir was a $50 million account! It was the only client that he'd kept aboard PPK when he launched his aggressive campaign to secure new and larger clients.

When he'd taken over Priest & King back in 1990, he immediately resigned every account the struggling agency maintained on its thin roster, except CorpAir. Duke and Princeton, along with their small staff of six thought that he'd completely lost his mind. But some thirty days later, CorpAir had already replaced half of the billings that were resigned by increasing their spending to $6 million a year. When Harvard bought the agency, CorpAir was a regional airline spending only $2 million a year on advertising, most of which was spent in various local newspapers.

PPK helped the airline to reposition themselves. Following the sole advice of Harvard, CorpAir revamped its marketing strategy and began catering exclusively to business travelers. The airline's planes were reconfigured and equipped with worktables. Business passengers were given access to fax and copy machines aboard each aircraft. There was even a small business library installed near the rear of the planes. Wall Street analysts would later dub the planes "the office in the sky".

Seemingly overnight, the strategy worked. CorpAir's growth was expeditious. New passengers were being added at a record-setting pace. The airline began offering service to major business cities within the U.S. and later added some key international markets, which included London and Hong Kong.

Three years after Harvard Prophet bought Priest & King, CorpAir's advertising expenditures had skyrocketed to an astonishing $20 million a year. The airline's new tagline, *Up Where You Belong,* was created by Harvard and quickly became one of the most memorable taglines ever created.

CorpAir's success garnered overwhelming media attention for Prophet, Priest & King - both locally and on a national level. However, like most successful ad agency clients, CorpAir became the object of PPK's competitors' affection.

It was five years ago that CorpAir first attempted to take their account away from PPK. Again, some newly appointed marketing chief thought that the airline had out-grown PPK. However, two weeks before several agencies were scheduled to make their final presentations to the CorpAir executive team, their marketing VP was attacked and killed while jogging near his suburban home late one evening. Harvard made an all-out effort to convince Douglas Sheldon to call off the entire review process. And to his surprise and delight, the review was postponed and never rescheduled.

Another storm front had been calmed.

Now, Harvard Prophet was determined to do whatever it took to ensure that his ten-year record of having never lost a client continued uninterrupted. "I'd be damned if I let you bastards walk away from this agency!" he mumbled to himself, his face twisted with anguish. He walked over and retrieved the letter from the floor. With his index finger trembling almost uncontrollably, he pressed the START button on his paper shredder. Within an instant, the *bearer* of bad news had been reduced to smithereens.

Harvard plopped down in the thick-padded, hunter-green leather chair that sat behind his desk. He grabbed hold of the telephone receiver with his left hand and proceeded to call his two minor partners – Duke Priest and Princeton King. They needed to haul their tails into the office pronto!

The chaos created by last night's stormy weather was mediocre in comparison to the developing storm that was about to hit the renowned advertising agency of *Prophet, Priest & King*.

CHAPTER THREE

HARVARD SAT ALONE IN HIS OFFICE nearly slumped over his desk. It hadn't quite approached the eight o'clock hour so there were no ringing phones clamoring for his attention, nor did he have to contend with repeated knocks at his door by those pleading for just a moment of his precious time.

Would there ever be an end to this madness, he contemplated to himself. This was now the second time that CorpAir wanted out. He would have thought that they'd learned their lesson after their last ill-fated attempt to place their account up for review.

Prophet, Priest & King had been a good home for CorpAir. Both the agency and client had garnered an impressive list of advertising awards within their ten-year marriage. Everyone - at least everyone that mattered - considered their relationship to be unique. It was a model by which other ad agencies sought to imitate. Clearly, PPK and CorpAir were a match made in advertising heaven.

Now it appeared that CorpAir had obviously been flirting with other possible suitors behind PPK's back. And Harvard would not tolerate infidelity. Neither would he entertain the thought of a separation of any kind. It was his agency that grew this account from practically nothing into a serious contender within the airline industry. The numbers of hours laboriously spent on this account alone were too numerous to even fathom.

Harvard closed his eyes and allowed the collage of memories to surface: the splashy magazine ads, the catchy radio jingles, and the mesmerizing television commercials had all made CorpAir a household name among business executives worldwide. It seemed everyone was singing the praises of CorpAir. And PPK was the irrefutable machine behind all that music. Indeed, all that glitter *was* gold.

Surely, Douglas Sheldon couldn't be serious about conducting this review. Didn't he understand that CorpAir's survival depended as much upon PPK as PPK depended upon CorpAir? And if he did understand it, then why was he choosing to tempt fate? It was quite clear to Harvard that CorpAir was perhaps simply infatuated with some other ad agency. Of course, he realized that it was an infatuation that couldn't be allowed to continue. It had to cease - immediately.

PPK has never allowed an account review to come to fruition within its ad agency. Harvard believed, unequivocally, that the very idea of such was totally and absolutely diametric to his principles and basic philosophy concerning the ad agency business. There were simply far too many ad agencies today that were failing miserably at keeping the accounts their agencies had fought so hard to win. And it wasn't due to a lack of good account management that accounted for these insurmountable losses. Harvard firmly believed that it was a lack of good *account leadership*.

The major difference between PPK and the others in the industry was that he assumed leadership on every single account that his agency maintained – whether it billed $1 million or $50 million. Harvard Prophet made it unmistakably clear that if an advertiser became his agency's account, then it was his agency that was in charge and not some power-hungry middle manager on the client side.

It was as simple as that.

After all, if the clients could chart their own course then why seek out an agency in the first place? The whole ad review process had frustrated Harvard more than he wanted to admit. It seemed the entire ad industry was being shot straight to hell by all these damn account reviews!

Enough was enough.

Whatever happened to *client loyalty*? Harvard hadn't realized it until now just how much the ad agency business had changed. So many ad agencies were finding themselves at the mercy of their clients. The almighty dollar was being dangled directly in front of their eyes and they were expected to perform silly tricks, or put on a rousing show of some sort. Perform well and a little more money was thrown your way. It was high-class prostitution in its finest hour. And sadly, it was legal as hell.

And just about anything nowadays could impel an account review. Harvard recalled the story that he'd heard from a colleague about an account review that was announced by the client within three weeks after the account had been awarded. Apparently, the CEO on the client side became ticked-off when he learned that the wife of the ad agency's president failed to speak to his wife at a local social event. And to add insult to injury, the incumbent agency wasn't even invited to participate in the review.

It was all insane.

Harvard Prophet refused to have any part of a client's *love 'em and leave 'em* shenanigans. He considered the ad agency-client relationship to be serious business. When a client formed a relationship with PPK, it would be nothing short of a long term and endearing relationship. He had absolutely no desire for one-night stands. Harvard believed that the agency chose the client just as importantly as the client chose the agency. And involved within that choice was a commitment - a vow. And to him it was a vow for life - an inseparable union.

Without a doubt, what his agency had joined together, he was not going to let anyone put asunder.

CHAPTER FOUR

A LONG AND CRISP WHITE-SLEEVED ARM was thrust between the two elevator doors just before the doors sealed in thirty-nine year-old PPK partner Duke Priest. Duke was patiently awaiting his ascension to the seventeenth floor of the Peachtree Towers office building. When the elevator doors smacked against the lone arm, they immediately retreated back inside the walls like two soldiers diligently obeying a Sergeant's command. And waiting outside the elevator stood Duke's counterpart Princeton King. At age thirty-seven, Princeton was the youngest of the three PPK agency principals.

"Thanks a lot!" Princeton greeted, as his Nike-clad feet stepped into the elevator. He was gripping his imitation leather brown attaché case in his right hand along with his suit jacket, while trying to massage his now sore left arm at the same time.

"Are you looking to donate a limb to medical research?" Duke remarked jokingly.

"Not hardly!" Princeton replied, quickly slipping into his signature red plaid jacket. "Although I'm not opposed to helping Emory University's aspiring med students with their anatomical studies. It's just that . . . well, the rest of my body wouldn't take too kindly to me freely disposing of one of their members."

Princeton reached over and pressed the CLOSE DOOR button on the side panel of the elevator. The two doors immediately reappeared from inside the walls and came together, sealing-in the two partners for their rapid ride up to the seventeenth floor.

"Well, if your remark is true," Duke began, "then I highly suggest that the next time you want to stop an elevator door from closing that you try sticking your brief-case between the doors instead of your arm," he politely advised.

"And ruin a five-hundred dollar attaché case!" Princeton exclaimed. "Never!"

Both men erupted into laughter. They knew that Princeton's attaché case had been bought from a street vendor several years ago who'd been selling them for a mere pittance along with several other items of fake brand-name merchandise.

It wasn't as if Princeton King couldn't afford an expensive piece of luggage to house the trappings of his job - after all, his fifteen percent share of PPK provided him with more than enough money to indulge in just about anything he desired. But Princeton cared little for extravagance. In fact, neither he nor Duke were spendthrifts. Before they relinquished control of their tiny and once carefree shop, they enjoyed the freedom of coming to work dressed in blue jeans and sneakers, or on some occasion even sandals.

On the surface Duke and Princeton were just a couple of ordinary gentlemen who'd migrated to the burgeoning south from Chicago in hopes of fulfilling their aspirations. Their dreams were built largely on their determination to take their small ad agency to great and lofty heights. But their failure to win major accounts resulted in their shop being labeled just a small creative boutique.

Collectively, the two men possessed enormous creative talent. What they lacked, however, was management finesse. When Harvard Prophet approached the cohorts about a possible buy-out, both men were surprised, to say the least. It wasn't as if the name Priest & King turned many heads within Atlanta's close-knit advertising community. But after some considerable thought, along with mounting financial obligations, the partners agreed to sell. They decided to retain a thirty percent share of the agency between them, although Harvard had bargained hard for one hundred percent ownership.

The reception area lay blanketed by darkness as Duke and Princeton stepped from the elevators. It was 7:45. Most of the agency's staff wouldn't start arriving until around 8:15. Harvard had summoned Duke and Princeton each on their cell phone. He minced few words as he demanded that they make their presence known within his office immediately. He refused to divulge specifics over the phone and neither partner pressed him. However, they both realized that something was up and it had to be anything but good news.

Although neither had ever admitted to it, Duke and Princeton unwillingly viewed Harvard Prophet as somewhat of a dominating father figure. And while they tried to give him the utmost respect when warranted, it wasn't always an easy thing to do. It was no secret that Harvard wanted both Duke and Princeton to sell their remaining interest in the agency to him. It wasn't enough that the old man clearly already had majority control of the agency; he felt the need to own all of it. Whether it was a major ego or power trip, neither Duke nor Princeton was able to ascertain.

Harvard's rapacious ambition was also palpable in the way he led the quest for new clients and his relentless determination to hold on to existing ones. Every review that PPK has been confronted with, the agency somehow was able to thwart the review and maintain its status as agency-of-record. And to date, no client has ever fired PPK. PPK is believed to be the only ad agency with such tenacious client staying power.

Princeton extended his sore arm and with his knuckles he tapped lightly on the polished mahogany door as the two men reached Harvard's office. Neither had stopped at his own office first.

"It's open!" they heard Harvard's imperious voice boom from inside his corner harborage.

Princeton cast an awkward glance at Duke before he reluctantly turned the brass door handle and slowly opened the door. He then quickly moved to one side, relegating to Duke the *privilege* of entering their boss' sanctuary first.

Harvard Prophet was sitting on the edge of his huge desk. His arms were folded tightly across his chest. His charcoal-gray suit jacket had been removed and his perfectly knotted silk tie had been loosened. He appeared deep in thought as he held his *Mont Blanc* fountain pen pressed firmly against his thin dry lips.

"Just have a seat, gentlemen," he instructed them, pointing to his burgundy leather sofa that was adjacent to his desk.

The two men assumed positions on the sofa, sitting inches apart from one another and with their attaché cases sitting squarely on their laps. Harvard walked over and stood tall before his two partners, towering above them like Goliath.

What's up?" Princeton uttered nervously.

"Just listen and you'll soon find out!" Harvard answered him tersely.

Duke and Princeton resented Harvard's many attempts to speak condescendingly to them. But neither had ever confronted him on the matter. They figured that since he primarily spoke that way to them in private they could live with it. Besides, they knew how much Harvard relished his majority control of the agency. Adding to that was the fact that he was also the oldest person among the three principals as well as the oldest person among the agency's youthful staff. This only seemed to augment his desire to play the dominant role.

Harvard stared precariously at his two partners. There were several instances when he opened his mouth to speak, but nothing came out. Duke and Princeton realized that whatever was on his mind, it had to be serious if it was rendering Harvard Prophet speechless.

"What's going on, Harvard?" Duke attempted to coax him.

Harvard breathed a heavy sigh before finally briefing his partners on the news that he'd received this morning from CorpAir.

"Did you have any idea this was coming? I mean, any warning signs?" Princeton asked, when the briefing was finished.

"Absolutely not!" Harvard shouted, still fuming inside.

"Incredible," Duke mumbled, scratching the bald spot atop his head. "What a way to kick-off our ten-year anniversary," he added, removing his attaché case from his lap and placing it on the round coffee table.

"Like hell it is!" Harvard bellowed. He walked over to the windows and stared down at the traffic once again.

"Well, at least we're invited to participate in the review," Princeton remarked, attempting to focus on the bright side.

Harvard turned from the windows and shot Princeton a menacing scowl. He responded to Princeton, "Need I remind you about my feelings on account reviews?"

Princeton quickly averted his eyes from the old man and began staring at the plush carpet beneath his feet. For a few seconds, though it seemed like minutes, no one said anything. They could hear the chatter of voices outside Harvard's office as PPK employees began arriving.

Duke removed his horn-rimmed glasses from his bearded face and began to wipe them with a white handkerchief he'd pulled from the hip pocket of his trousers. He tried to digest the impact that the loss of a $50 million account would have on the agency. There would undoubtedly be layoffs. They would probably even have to move to much smaller office space considering that their seventeenth floor haven was costing them a fortune in monthly rent.

Duke snuck a glance at the old man, who now appeared as a blur to him without his eyeglasses on. Duke knew that Harvard Prophet deserved immense credit. He practically single-handedly built PPK into an advertising force to be reckoned with. Harvard prided himself on the fact that not one client had ever been lost by the agency. But Duke always knew that such an impressive achievement couldn't continue indefinitely. The very nature of the advertising agency business dictated that accounts come and go. Of course, Harvard Prophet wasn't a man accustomed to losing. Duke and Princeton would later find out that Harvard's life-long quest had been to own an ad agency. And for someone who'd never worked at an ad agency a single day in his entire life, he had ambitiously created a powerhouse shop in Atlanta.

On at least five separate occasions PPK had been approached by much larger agencies seeking an acquisition. Harvard never entertained their offers. He wanted no part of this sad trend. In fact, he had lofty goals of his own. Over the past year he'd been contemplating the purchase of a New York shop to establish a *Madison Avenue* presence for PPK. Duke realized now that those ambitious pursuits would have to be placed on the back burner. Much farther back on the burner. This account review would become the hottest thing cooking for Prophet, Priest & King over the summer.

Princeton stared at the white Nike sneakers covering his feet. He'd tried unsuccessfully to resist Harvard's implementation of a corporate dress code for the agency, which mandated suits and ties for the men. Princeton had argued with Harvard the fact that as the Creative Director for the agency he couldn't keep his creative juices flowing if he was suited up all day. The argument fell upon deaf ears. After heated confrontations between them and Princeton's vain attempt at dispelling threats to resign, he found himself acquiescing to Harvard. Of course, it was only after Harvard had invoked his powers as majority stockholder. However, Princeton refused to wear dress shoes. He gave Harvard some flimsy excuse about recurring problems with his feet not being able to breathe in dress shoes, and how that sneakers were the only comfort given to his often-aching feet. The old man had grunted some obscenities to him and then ordered him to keep a pair of dress shoes in his office just in case a client dropped by the premises unannounced. So, with every jacket and tie he wore to work, Princeton King could be seen gleefully sporting his signature red plaid jacket and white high-top sneakers.

Princeton soon began to fiddle with the tie around his neck. He could sure use a drink. He realized that he wasn't supposed to be thinking about alcohol ever since his wife had made him promise to quit drinking several years ago. "For the kids' sake," she'd argued with him on numerous occasions.

Princeton's thoughts quickly gave way to his two lovely children - an eight year-old daughter and a two year-old son. They were definitely the pride of his life. He couldn't imagine his children growing up apart from their father. It was that distinct possibility that kept him fighting assiduously his temptation to drink. If Muriel left him again he realized that it would probably be for good this time.

Princeton tried to erase the disturbing thought of his wife packing up the children's belongings along with her own and loading them into her silver Volvo wagon and driving back north to Chicago. The mental image began to blur from the pain starting to surface. He made an abrupt detour from that line of thinking and re-directed his thoughts again to the crisis at hand.

He had seen the handwriting on the wall for this review. It was inevitable. Happened all the time. Harvard shouldn't take it so personally. Princeton figured that CorpAir had simply outgrown them. And in all fairness to the airline, he realized that the review was perhaps nothing more than a business decision. They all knew that CorpAir had been planning some sort of a marketing alliance with a major international carrier. Once that deal became cemented, it would have only been a matter of time before CorpAir would have sought the affiliation of one of the big New York shops to spearhead their new marketing thrust. The problem was that Harvard had wrongfully assumed that PPK would be the one to benefit from their client's aggressive marketing goals.

Despite the fact that PPK was participating in the review, Princeton personally believed that CorpAir was allowing their participation only as a matter of courtesy. The chances of PPK actually keeping this account were nil.

"When will the first round of presentations start?" Duke inquired.

Harvard took a seat in his big fat leather chair. "Don't know a damn thing more than what was in the letter," he muttered, unable to hide the fact that he was visibly shaken by CorpAir's bombshell.

"May I see the fax?" Duke asked.

"No. I shredded it," Harvard answered matter-of-factly.

"You did what?" Princeton shouted, taking the words right out of Duke's mouth.

"You heard me."

"What was your purpose in doing that?" Princeton pressed.

"Maybe because I felt the hell like it!" Harvard replied, his words vociferating. "Do you have a problem with my actions?"

Princeton seemed to sink deeper into the burgundy sofa as he slowly nodded his head to indicate that he did not have a problem with the old man's actions.

"Good. I didn't think you would," Harvard snapped back. "Now here's where we stand. I'm expecting a call from Douglas at any moment. And when he does call I intend to fully communicate to him, in no uncertain terms, my absolute dissatisfaction with this absurd course of action."

Duke and Princeton sat quietly as their boss continued his enthralling and expletive-laden speech. Neither partner dared to interrupt. Harvard Prophet was on a roll. Silently, they each wished for Douglas Sheldon's phone call to come quickly and put an end to Harvard's soapbox antics.

As CEO for CorpAir, Douglas Sheldon held a deep admiration for Harvard. Over the years their business relationship had evolved into an enviable friendship. Douglas, much younger than Harvard, admired him for his uncanny tenacity. He appreciated Harvard's business voracity. He'd often stated that Harvard was a natural-born genius when it came to creativity.

Douglas and Harvard often golfed together at the private Golf Club of the South. They both played well enough to keep a competitive rivalry going between them. They also participated in several charitable golf tournaments held throughout the year. It was precisely because of their close relationship that this untimely news of the review was more upsetting to Harvard. He would have at least expected a private meeting with Douglas Sheldon beforehand.

Harvard's phone buzzed, startling Duke and Princeton. He grabbed at it quickly and nervously. "Harvard Prophet," he answered. "You've dialed the wrong office," he told the caller, sighing. "You want *Seymour Boudreau*. He's the media director. Call back and ask for him!" He slammed the telephone receiver back onto the console. "When are we going to get this damn receptionist problem fixed!" he barked.

Princeton quickly offered up a response. "We've got a girl coming in today for an interview," he told him.

"Not good enough!" Harvard retorted. "I want someone *hired* today! And get rid of those incompetent temps! My god, I've rerouted more calls these past few weeks than an AT&T operator!"

"I understand," Princeton apologized. "Lorraine and I are on top of the situation," he added, referring to Lorraine Brown, PPK's office manager.

"You damn-well better be! And consider hiring a *male* receptionist!" Harvard spouted. "At least we won't have to worry about him taking *maternity* leave!"

Princeton allowed the old man's instructions to go unheeded. He and Lorraine had already scheduled a promising interview with a young woman who was an advertising student at *The Portfolio Institute* – a creative advertising school in Atlanta for anxious students aspiring to get ad agency jobs as copywriters, art directors, illustrators or some other creative post.

Duke arose from the sofa and walked toward Harvard's desk. Duke was a short, stocky man, measuring five-feet-three. "What would you like for me to do," he asked.

"There's not much any of us can do at the moment until I hear from Douglas," he answered firmly. "However, you might want to prepare to contact all the other clients and inform them of this situation before they read about it in the press. Lord knows, once news of this review breaks, rumors and innuendoes regarding this agency's future are going to be running rampant!"

"Yeah, I suppose you're right," Duke replied. "We do stand to lose half the agency's billings - more than enough to not only send shock waves across our entire client roster, but enough to start a ripple effect as well."

"Tell me something that I don't already know," Harvard growled.

As Duke made his way toward the door, Princeton quickly grabbed his attaché case and followed pursuit.

"Wait a minute, gentlemen," Harvard's voice stopped them at the door. They turned their attention to him. "Any calls from the press regarding this matter and I want them referred to my office, understood?"

Both men shook their head in agreement.

"And make sure your subordinates are briefed. I don't want to see anyone panicking. Tell them everything is business as usual. And that includes our anniversary celebration tonight at the *Marriott Marquis*."

Duke and Princeton made mental notes of Harvard's instructions before turning and hurrying out the door.

CHAPTER FIVE

ADIVA ROBERTS WAS NOTICEABLY nervous as she dressed in the upstairs bathroom of the two-bedroom, two-story home where she lived with her eighty-three year-old grandmother, Granny Rae. Adiva had an eleven o'clock interview with one of Atlanta's most talked about advertising agencies. She considered the interview a once-in-a-lifetime opportunity. A career in advertising was her dream. It was an industry where she knew she'd been born to thrive.

Granted, the job being offered was only that of a *receptionist*. But Adiva knew that in this business you got your foot into the door by whatever means you could. After all, she could not afford to be choosy – especially since it seemed that the doors didn't open too often for black females. She intended to take full advantage of this interview. This job could very well be her springboard to what she hoped would be a promising and prosperous career as an advertising copywriter. She was scheduled to graduate this fall, although her classes had already ended. It had been two very long years that she'd spent at The Portfolio Institute. Attending classes all day Mondays through

Thursdays and a half-day on Fridays, for eight straight quarters, had taken its toll on her petite body.

Adiva stared mirthfully at her diminutive reflection in the full-length oval-shaped mirror that hung on the wall behind the bathroom door. At twenty-five years of age, she was no more than five-feet tall. She wore a dress size of one. Her fair-skinned, permanently tanned body endured a rigorous workout twice a week at the health gym. She ate no red meat. Her lily-white teeth were perfect, displaying a smile that could easily weaken the strongest of men. And she kept her hair cut very short and feathered. It had been dyed a honey-blonde shade. She'd been told that she resembled *Jada Pinkett-Smith* on many occasions.

Ever since she was three years old, Granny Rae had raised Adiva. It had been an awesome task, considering that Granny Rae was sixty-years-old at the time. Adiva's parents were killed in a plane crash twenty-two years ago. They were returning home to Birmingham, Alabama from a vacation in Miami when the commuter plane on which they were traveling went down just outside of Macon, Georgia. Her parents were scheduled to connect with a major carrier in Atlanta. Adiva was supposed to have accompanied her parents on the trip, but an unrelenting fever precluded her from going. Granny Rae had driven to Birmingham from her Atlanta home to take care of her only grandchild. Of course, she had no idea at the time that her granddaughter would eventually spend the next several years under her direct guardianship. The commuter airline awarded a fairly decent monetary settlement to Granny Rae on Adiva's behalf. The money afforded Adiva the privilege of attending a private Christian school in Atlanta. There were also enough funds to send her to Georgia State University without the assistance of student loans. The last of the settlement money had been spent two years ago when Adiva paid the full tuition to enroll at The Portfolio Institute.

Now, Adiva Roberts needed a job. Granny Rae's home had been paid off with the proceeds that she'd received from her husband's life insurance. Adiva never knew her grandfather. He died from a heart attack two years before Adiva was born. So, even with the house debt-free, there were still other necessary living expenses constantly demanding attention - utilities, food, car insurance premiums and various prescription medications for Granny Rae.

For about as long as she could remember, Adiva felt that she was spending more of her time caring for Granny Rae. And since her grandmother was unable to move about without the assistance of a walker, Adiva converted a spare room downstairs into a bedroom for Granny Rae so that she wouldn't have to worry about trying to climb the stairs. Granny Rae had fought her granddaughter's efforts to spend most of her time caring for her well being. But she could never quite convince Adiva that she was capable of doing most things by herself. Besides, Granny Rae was the only family member that Adiva had. Their relationship was endearing.

Adiva glanced at her watch. It was 10:15. She knew that she needed to put a move on it. Their house, nestled on a quiet street in a Sandy Springs subdivision comprised of only thirty homes, was probably a good twenty minutes away from PPK's offices.

Adiva began to scrutinize the vast array of lipsticks she had sprawled across the counter of her bathroom sink. There appeared to be every shade of the Revlon collection and she was trying to decide which to wear. Finally, she selected a Martinique Mauve. It would go well with her Regal Wine nail polish, she concluded. Adiva hurriedly applied the lipstick to her trembling lips. She was becoming more and more nervous as the hour of her interview approached. She heard the telephone ring. It only rang twice before Granny Rae's voice, straining to achieve volume, came crackling from downstairs.

"Diva! Diva! The telephone's for you!" Adiva heard her grandmother shouting. "I think it's that *soup fella*!" she shouted again, referring to Adiva's boyfriend Soupa Mann.

"Granny Rae, tell Soupa Mann that I'll call him back later!" Adiva yelled in return. She knew that her grandmother would be delighted to tell Soupa Mann that he couldn't talk to her right now. Granny Rae cared very little for Soupa Mann. One reason was due to the fact that Soupa Mann was thirty-eight years-old, divorced and had a twelve-year-old son living in California.

Soupa Mann insisted that people address him by his *first* and *last* name. It sounded much better than just *Soupa.* He worked as a Maintenance Technician at CorpAir's hangar at the Atlanta Southfield International Airport. When Adiva once tried to explain to her grandmother that Soupa Mann's job involved preparing the CorpAir planes for travel, Granny Rae had insisted on details about exactly what that meant. Adiva explained to her that Soupa Mann did everything from vacuum the planes and service the onboard fax and copy machines, to putting new trash liners in the wastebaskets. Of course, Granny Rae had remarked, "sounds like he ain't nothin' but a janitor!" But Adiva knew that her boyfriend was much more than that. Soupa Mann was also an aspiring singer. And he was quite good at it. He performed routinely at various clubs around Atlanta.

Adiva stole one last peek at her appearance in the mirror before she grabbed her purse from the dresser and quickly descended the stairs.

"Why you all prettied-up, Diva?" Granny Rae asked when Adiva came into the den. Granny Rae was sitting on the sofa watching reruns of *Little House On The Prairie.* Her arthritic hands, involuntarily decorated with age-spots, were folded and resting on her lap. Not a trace of gray hair could be found among her thousands of black strands, which were tied in two long ponytails that hung loosely on each side of her head, barely gracing the top of her hunching shoulders.

"I have a job interview, Granny Rae," Adiva answered.

"You ain't tell me nothin' 'bout no job, Diva," Granny Rae uttered, her feelings wounded. After all, her granddaughter usually shared everything with her.

"They just called me on Friday, Granny Rae. Didn't I mention something to you?" Adiva asked rhetorically, as she began a frantic search for her car keys.

Granny Rae thought for a moment, her memory still sharper than ever. "Naw, you ain't tell me nothin' 'bout no interview. 'Cause I'd 'member if you had," she answered Adiva.

"Well, it's with an advertising agency," Adiva sighed. "I'll tell you all about it when I get back, Granny Rae." She found her car keys between the stuffed cushions at the opposite end of the sofa from where her grandmother was sitting. "Okay, I gotta run, Granny Rae." Adiva leaned over and kissed her grandmother's soft, but sagging cheeks. The wounded look in Granny Rae's pensive eyes pierced Adiva's heart. Leaving her grandmother alone was never an easy task. She often wished that she could take her along whenever she left the house. But her grandmother's stroke a few years ago made it nearly impossible for her to do much of anything.

"Remember, don't try and climb those stairs," Adiva admonished her, after kissing her pendulous cheeks a second time.

Granny Rae's eyes followed her granddaughter's every move until she finally disappeared out the front door. She listened intently. A quiet roar was heard once the ignition started on Adiva's car. It wasn't until after Adiva had driven away that Granny Rae resumed interest in *Laura Ingalls* and her family.

Harvard Prophet cursed repeatedly within the four walls of his office as he stared blankly at the front page of this week's edition of Advertising Age magazine. The headline, in large black bold type, read: **ATLANTA-BASED CORPAIR PUTS $50 MILLION ACCOUNT UP FOR REVIEW.** And just below the headline, the subhead read: *Incumbent Agency's Future Is Uncertain.*

Those sneaky bastards! They've known about this all along! Harvard's blood pressure began rising faster than the mercury on a thermometer in the Phoenix desert. He was still awaiting a call from CorpAir's CEO Douglas Sheldon. He'd decided that he would give Douglas until eleven o'clock to return his call before he would personally storm their damn offices.

When Harvard's secretary brought the morning mail to his office, the Advertising Age cover story stood out like a sore thumb. And the phones were yet to stop ringing. PPK was being inundated with calls from the across the country - from industry trade writers to local reporters. Harvard was forced to instruct his secretary to hold all of his calls with the exception of any calls from CorpAir - especially if the call was from Douglas Sheldon.

Harvard scanned the magazine article again for the umpteenth time. CorpAir's new vice president of marketing, Christine Armstrong, was quoted at length throughout the front page news story. He wanted to wring her bony little neck. The article was littered with information that he should have been made aware of *before* the review was announced publicly.

"How unprofessional," he mumbled. Harvard learned from the article that the agencies would begin making their initial presentations in less than thirty days, with final presentations due in August. It was emphasized that PPK was the only non-New York agency participating in the review. He was a bit surprised by the presence of the billion-dollar ad agencies. He grunted as he reviewed the list of contenders again. He couldn't believe that they were actually vying for *his* account. PPK was a mere guppy as compared to those advertising sharks! Was it that difficult drumming up new business on Madison Avenue?

"Greedy bastards!" Harvard cursed aloud. He knew that he couldn't allow those big agency vultures to prey upon what rightfully belonged to Prophet, Priest & King. He suspected that one of them, or perhaps even all of them, must have been wooing CorpAir for quite some time - behind his back of course. Unfortunately, it was an all too common practice these days. Harvard figured he'd just have to pull out all the stops on this one. The very future of his agency depended upon it. Hell, his life depended upon it.

Harvard's secretary buzzed his phone.

"Yes, Elizabeth?" he answered. "Thank you. Put him through!" It was Douglas Sheldon. Harvard stood from his desk and depressed the button for the speakerphone. He quickly removed the platinum cuff links from his white crisply-starched shirt and rolled up both sleeves.

"Good morning, Harv! How the hell are you?" Douglas greeted him with a cachinnate laugh.

"I think you know damn well how I'm doing, Douglas!" Harvard answered angrily, his contention growing with every second.

Douglas pretended to know nothing of the sort. "Missed you out on the links this morning, Harv. Can you believe that I shot a seventy-two! I tell you Harv the greens were smoother than a baby's bottom - despite all that rain last night. But the grounds crew did one heck of . . . "

"Don't be coy with me, Douglas!" Harvard interrupted him. "You know damn well that I haven't been trying to reach you all morning to discuss your self-applauding golf game! Or the weather for that matter!"

Douglas Sheldon's grin quickly diminished. "Hey, lighten-up Harv. What's eatin' you?"

"Dammit, Douglas!" Harvard shouted, banging his fist against the desk. "We've been friends for a very long time. Now I deserve some sort of an explanation! And don't placate me!"

"Well, do you mind clueing me in as to why you're ranting and raving?"

Harvard exhaled fiercely. "As if you don't already know!"

Harvard paused, nodding his head incredulously. "I'm talking about the lousy fax sent to me last night by your new VP announcing this review, Douglas! Is this how you're going to start treating our friendship?"

"Aw hell, Harv. Is that what you're up in arms about? Accounts are placed in review all the time - surely you know that!"

"Not at my agency, Douglas!"

Douglas emitted a raspy chuckle. "Didn't we invite you guys to participate in the review as well?"

"Of course, Douglas. But that's the least I would have expected."

"Listen, Harv. You fellas do some great stuff over there. Now, my advice to you is that you put every damn thing you've got into your presentation. Leave no stone unturned. We are going to give consideration to every contender."

"Don't feed me that crap, Douglas! You've got us competing with billion-dollar agencies! There's no way in hell that we can match their budgets!" Harvard argued.

The near-bushy eyebrows on Douglas Sheldon's forehead arched upward. "Since when has Harvard Prophet ever been afraid of Madison Avenue?"

"You listen to me, Douglas! I'm going to be ingenuous with you. I do not want to waste my agency's time and resources pitching an account that we may not have a snowball's-chance-in-hell of winning back!"

Douglas sighed. "Well, Harv. I can't tell you how to run your business over there. But like I said, CorpAir is going to give full consideration to every participant in this review. You have my word on that."

Harvard rattled off some more curses. He stopped short of withdrawing PPK from the review altogether. Before terminating the conversation he made it a point to remind Douglas Sheldon of how PPK had stood by CorpAir over the years. He also emphasized how he himself single-handedly devised the strategy that created a niche market for CorpAir.

Of course, Douglas spouted many heart-felt thanks. He likewise reminded Harvard of how CorpAir had helped PPK to gain renowned praise throughout the advertising world. Both men were reluctant to bow to pressure from the other. And as their conversation drew to a close, Douglas Sheldon paused briefly during his concluding remarks. Harvard waited while the CEO made three attempts to clear his throat of an unknown ailment.

"Excuse me," he uttered, finally clearing his throat. "By the way, Harv," he began as he concluded the call. "Happy tenth anniversary!"

Harvard stiffened as the words penetrated his ears. The absence of adulation in Douglas' voice was unmistakable. He failed to see any humor in Douglas' apparent sarcasm. In that precise moment, Harvard Prophet resented - no, he despised his major client. CorpAir was deriving some sort of subtle pleasure from announcing this review at a time when they should have been joining with PPK to celebrate their ten-year union. But over the years Harvard had come to realize that many clients savored the immense power and control afforded them by virtue of the size of their advertising budgets. The bigger the budgets, the more control they sought to exercise.

Harvard stared blankly at the telephone console. He knew that he was as much a factor for CorpAir's success as Douglas Sheldon was being credited with. They were nothing before PPK took them on as a client. Their effect on the airline industry was minuscule at best. Not even a ripple in the pond. In fact, CorpAir was on the verge of being gobbled up by WesternSky Airlines and having their image all but done away with. Yet, Harvard devised a marketing strategy for them that would forever alter their course of business. His reward for such had been the exclusive agency-of-record status for the airline. And rightly so.

Now, everything had been placed in jeopardy. And why? *Power* and *control.* CorpAir indeed has the ability to totally yank their $50 million account from PPK and place it squarely in the hands of another ad agency. And within an instant, his agency - his lifeblood - would be relegated to the minor leagues. A league he refused to play in. The loss of CorpAir would mean the loss of scores of jobs. Relationships that had been built over many years would be severed. Families perhaps ruined. Talent squandered. And why? All because CorpAir, like so many other advertisers, wanted to exercise the power and control that was sitting shamefully at their disposal. *Somebody* had to put an end to this utter madness once and for all. It was time that an ad agency stood up to reclaim its power and its glory.

Prophet, Priest & King would have to become that somebody.

Glory, glory hallelujah!

CHAPTER SIX

THIRTY-FIVE YEAR-OLD LORRAINE BROWN couldn't keep herself from silently scrutinizing Adiva Roberts' appearance as Adiva sat directly across from her at the small round conference table. Half of what Adiva had been speaking about during their interview had gone into one of Lorraine's ears and out the other. Adiva, however, was relieved that her first interview was with a *sister*. It help to put her mind at ease.

Throughout the interview, which had been going on for some twenty minutes, Adiva sensed that Lorraine was seriously checking her out from top to bottom. Finally, unable to refrain any longer, Lorraine broached the delicate subject. "Your hair looks . . . well, it's *different*," she stammered.

Adiva stared at her for a moment.

"Different in what way?" She asked Lorraine.

Lorraine began to fidget. "Well, it's just that . . . you know . . . I mean, the color," she attempted to explain.

"The color?" Adiva echoed. "Is there a problem with it or something?"

Lorraine displayed a half-hearted smile. "Well, Miss Roberts, you do realize that you're being considered for a receptionist position? And of course, this is a very professional environment . . . well, do you understand what I'm trying to say?"

Adiva had been sitting upright in her chair. Her hands were clasped together and resting on her lap. She unclasped them, tilted her body to the right and folded her arms across her chest. "No, Ms. Brown. I don't understand what you're trying to say. And yes, I am aware of the position that I'm being interviewed for. But how does my hair have anything to do with that?"

Lorraine forced a laugh. "C'mon girlfriend," she began. "Do you really expect me to believe that this is your *natural* hair color?"

Remain cool and calm. This wasn't the time or place to go off. *Get behind me Satan!*

"I am not here to make you believe anything. But since you seem to be fascinated with my hair, you might want to do something about those split-ends of yours," Adiva retorted, her teeth clenching.

"Excuse me?"

"Surely you understand what I'm trying to say?" Adiva mocked. "I mean, girlfriend your hair is splitting up faster than a Hollywood marriage, okay?"

Lorraine, quite self-conscious now, began to grasp strands of her long jet-black hair. Adiva was pleased to see that she'd succeeded at rattling her. "We're not talking about me, Miss Roberts," Lorraine responded. "What I suggest is that if you're serious about working for this agency, you consider losing the

Dennis Rodman look – this is an ad agency, not the NBA."

Adiva couldn't believe what she was hearing. Who was this bumpy-face, weave wearing, glorified administrative assistant trying to give beauty advice? She wanted to reach across the conference table and yank that piece of horse's hair right off Lorraine's arrogant head. Apparently, she intimidated the home girl. It was so infantile. But Adiva had no intentions of allowing this woman, who obviously knew nothing about her, to get under her skin.

"Didn't I see a guy with *red* hair walking around here?" Adiva questioned.

"You may have. However, that red-haired gentleman is one of the principals in this agency. And as a matter of fact, you were scheduled to meet with him next," Lorraine stated, being careful to emphasize the word *were*.

"Still, why is it okay to have red hair and not honey-blonde in this professional environment?"

"Miss Roberts, at the risk of repeating myself, Princeton King is an agency principal, not the receptionist. And besides, he was born with his hair color. Now, can we say the same about yours?"

Adiva's cool quickly melted.

"What I was born with Ms. Brown is the freedom to choose to do what I want. I was also taught good manners, like how to speak pleasantly with someone and to maintain a respectful attitude. Can we say the same about your rude and nasty attitude?" Having stated her mind, Adiva promptly got up from her chair. She realized that her chances of getting this job had melted just as quickly as her cool had. She politely thanked Lorraine for her time and turned to exit the premises when Lorraine spoke.

"Sit down, Miss Roberts - please," she said. "Let's not be hasty."

Slowly and with much reserve in her step, Adiva returned to her seat.

"Perhaps we can make an exception to the hair thing." She said this because she realized that Adiva Roberts was PPK's last viable candidate for the job. And the pressure was being put on her to hire someone immediately.

"Then why did you make a big deal of my hair?" Adiva asked.

"I may have gone a little overboard," Lorraine gave an obligatory answer. "The fact-of-the matter is, I like you. So, if I offended you, then please accept my apology."

Adiva nodded and smiled back at her guardedly.

The two women continued the interview process. Adiva wanted to know if there were any other African-Americans working at PPK.

"Let me see . . ." Lorraine thought aloud, tapping her pen lightly against her right cheek. "There's a black accounting assistant in the finance department," she told Adiva. Lorraine thought some more. "One of our art directors is also black. And, let's see . . . oh yeah we have one black account supervisor."

"Is that all?" Adiva asked in disappointment. "Didn't you say earlier that PPK has over one hundred employees?"

"That's correct."

"And you only have *three* African-Americans on staff?"

"Well, *four,* counting me," Lorraine corrected her.

Adiva shook her head disapprovingly.

"Oh, I almost forgot," Lorraine added. "There's also *Seymour Boudreau.* Now, the man's *skin* is black. But he was actually born and raised in Paris – I think his mother is French and his father is African-American."

"What's his position?" Adiva asked simply out of curiosity.

"Seymour is our VP of Media. He's the highest-ranking minority in the agency. And of course, let me tell you, he brown-noses big time to Mr. Prophet – but let's keep that between you and I," she sneered.

"Sounds like an interesting place to work," Adiva remarked.

"Well, like any other agency, we do have our moments."

The two women discussed the relevant details of the position. Adiva wanted to know what happened to the previous receptionist. Lorraine explained to her that she went on maternity leave back in April and once the baby was born she decided to become a full-time mom. Lorraine also shared with Adiva how PPK had gone through several receptionists from various temporary employment firms over the past three months. Practically every week a different face would be seen sitting at the front desk. This, she further explained, was driving Harvard Prophet insane, especially since numerous calls were inadvertently routed to his office.

Adiva's next interview was with PPK partner Princeton King. As she sat in his cluttered office awaiting his return, she noticed several photo boards lying atop his hunter-green rectangular shaped desk. She was curious as to what television commercial the still photographs had been prepared for. Simply glancing at the photo boards gave Adiva a sudden rush of adrenaline. She anxiously awaited the day when she could be involved in the creation of glossy magazine ads or memorable TV commercials. She looked forward to the demands that would be showered upon her to produce ad copy for a major client's campaign. She imagined being locked in a conference room pulling an all-nighter with other creative staffers - brainstorming while they munched on cold pizza and drank warm sodas. And at the eleventh hour, after having been emotionally drained and physically exhausted, the winning advertising campaign would finally be conceived. Their arduous efforts would be rewarded with huge bonuses and numerous industry awards.

Adiva sat up straight in the chair when she heard the handle turn on the door. When it opened she saw the familiar red head that she'd seen earlier while waiting in the reception area.

"I apologize for having kept you waiting," Princeton King said to her before taking a seat behind his desk. He leaned back in his chair, locked his hands together behind his head and then plopped his size twelve sneakers on top of his desk. Adiva could only stare awkwardly at this *professional* sitting across from her.

"So, what do you think about Prophet, Priest & King thus far?" he immediately threw out the first question.

Adiva tried to relax but she could feel her hands perspiring. "Well, it seems like a great place to work," she answered, praying that her nervousness would remain hidden.

"What makes you say that?" Princeton continued.

Because I couldn't think of a better answer, she wanted to say. "Well, from what I've learned about the agency from my interview with Ms. Brown as well as my own background research, you do excellent work. You also have an enviable client roster, and right now you're one of the hottest ad agencies in the country," Adiva stated, becoming more relaxed.

Princeton began to run his fingers through his hair, which Adiva noticed was more of a russet than red. "I see," he replied, as he opened one of the drawers on the credenza behind his desk and pulled out a small orange *Nerf* basketball and began dribbling it on his desk – occasionally hoisting it into the air as if he was *Larry Bird* attempting a three-pointer. "You're an ad student at The Portfolio Institute, right?" he asked, scanning her resume.

"Yes," Adiva answered. "Actually, I've already completed my required classes. The only thing left for me to do before I graduate is to write a report on something involving advertising."

Princeton nodded his head. "What did you study?"

"Copywriting."

"I see. Interested in the creative side of the business, huh?"

Adiva smiled demurely. "Well, I would like to think that I have a creative flair when it comes to writing."

Princeton returned a cursory smile. "I got my start as a copywriter at *J. Walter Baxter* in Chicago several years ago. Best place I've ever worked." There was a brief pause, as he appeared to be reminiscing about his early days in the agency business. Adiva was somewhat familiar with JWB – it was one of the larger agencies headquartered in New York with branch offices all over.

"Tell me how you became interested in advertising?" Princeton's questions continued.

This was the one question that she hoped would not be asked. She could feel the sweat begin a slow drip beneath her arms. Adiva wasn't sure if she should be candid or not. It wasn't the question itself that stifled her. It was the answer that she was embarrassed about revealing.

"Well . . . " she began, fidgeting somewhat. "I'm kind of embarrassed to say this – but ever since I was ten years old I've enjoyed watching television episodes of *Bewitched* . . . "

Princeton quickly slid his feet from atop his desk and leaned in closer across his desk, as if Adiva was about to reveal Coca-Cola's secret formula.

" . . . And well, you know – *Samantha Stevens'* husband *Darren* portrayed an advertising account executive at *McMann & Tate*. And um, I used to get so excited watching him come up with ad slogans that one day I took a can of *Campbell's Soup* from my grandmother's kitchen and set it on the table and stared at it for hours trying to come up with my own slogan for *Campbell's Soup* . . . "

Adiva couldn't continue because Princeton, unable to contain himself, had burst into an infectious roar of laughter. "And I thought *I* was the only one who had ever done that sort of thing," he finally admitted through his laughter.

Adiva was relieved that Princeton King was able to see the humor in all of this. She continued,

"Ever since then, I've been fascinated with advertising. I mean, sometimes I find myself more interested in the television commercials than the programs!"

"Same here," Princeton chuckled. "Of course, Adiva, you do realize that the position we're seeking to fill is that of a receptionist?"

"Yes, I understand."

Princeton ran his fingers through his hair again. "So tell me then, how is that going to figure in with your creative aspirations?"

"Well, I realize that a person has to start somewhere. And since I've never worked in an ad agency before, I feel that I can learn a lot from this position."

Princeton scribbled some notes on the yellow legal pad that was lying alongside Adiva's resume. "Tell me all that you know about PPK?" he quizzed her.

Adiva exhaled slowly. "Well, as I mentioned earlier, I know that you're one of the hottest agencies in the country. You've won numerous awards for your advertising work. Your largest client is the CorpAir account and I believe that you have annual billings around $80 million."

"$100 million," Princeton corrected her. Although he realized that with the CorpAir account now in jeopardy, that figure could be changing drastically.

Adiva continued to rattle off facts that she'd learned about the ad agency from her routine reading of Advertising Age and Adweek magazines. Her nervousness had subsided. She found Princeton King an easy person to converse with. She could definitely see herself working for this man - much more than she could see herself working for Lorraine Brown. Although the sister had apologized for her obnoxious behavior, Adiva realized that she'd still have to watch her back where Lorraine was concerned.

Princeton finished jotting down the last of his notes. He put his pen down and plopped his feet back onto his desk. "So Adiva, how would you like to become PPK's new receptionist?"

Adiva's heartbeat began to accelerate. "Excuse me? I mean, are you offering me the job?"

"Provided you can start tomorrow morning at 8:00 sharp!"

"Um . . .sure, no problem."

"Then allow me to be the first to welcome you to the Prophet, Priest & King family!" Princeton stood and stretched his arm across the desk to shake Adiva's hand.

"Thank you Mr. King!"

"Uh, call me Princeton."

"Thank you, Princeton. I really appreciate this opportunity."

"Adiva, I do want you to understand that I cannot make any promises as to when you might be able to move from this position to the creative side."

Adiva nodded affirmatively. "I understand."

"However," he added. "If you can prove yourself with our challenging phone system, then I will personally do all that I can to try and find a spot for you where you'll be able to utilize your creative skills – fair enough?"

"Yes. Again, thank you so much Mr. Ki . . . um, Princeton."

Princeton covered some preliminary issues with Adiva and instructed her that she would be meeting with the VP of Human Resources to complete all the necessary paperwork. After he'd given her final instructions he moved from his desk and began to escort her toward the door. "Our VP of Human Resources' office is down the hall and just to the left of the library," he told her pointing down the corridor.

"I'm very grateful for this opportunity, Princeton. You've made my day!"

Princeton smiled politely. "By the way, Adiva," he called out to her as she exited his office. "Love that hair color!"

◈◈◈◈◈◈◈

Princeton King ate his lunch behind the closed doors of his office today. Usually he ate downstairs in the building's first floor cafeteria. As he licked the white cream filling from the chocolate cupcake off his fingers, he developed an intense thirst. It was no ordinary thirst that could be easily quenched with a few gulps of ice-cold water. Princeton allowed his imagination to conjure up a tall frosty mug of beer. Subconsciously, he began to lick his lips as he imagined the white foam spilling slowly over the top of the glass. This hallucination continued for another ten minutes before Princeton had driven himself crazy thinking about a beer.

He jumped from his chair and raced over to the two-drawer lateral file cabinet that stood in the corner of his office and yanked open the bottom drawer. Inside was a small cooler - just big enough to maintain a six-pack. Princeton lifted the top from the cooler. Immediately his eyes became fixed on the cans of cold brew that were surrounded by square chunks of ice. He hesitated before seizing one of the cans. He ripped it open and drank it hastily, spilling some of the beer onto his tie. Satisfied that the beer can was empty - bone dry - he repeated the insatiable act with a second can. The brew was refreshing.

After the second can had been emptied, Princeton placed both empty beer cans on the floor and stomped on them with his sneakers until they were as flat as a pancake. He then retrieved a large ten by thirteen plain manila envelope from his supply drawer and placed the two flattened cans inside. He carefully dumped the contents of his wastebasket onto the floor. Then he wadded up the manila envelope as best he could and placed it at the bottom of the wastebasket. The other trash was then put back into the wastebasket - essentially covering up what had become Princeton King's private and forbidden little rendezvous.

CHAPTER SEVEN

IT WAS NOT QUITE 7:30 WHEN ADIVA Roberts arrived to work the following Tuesday morning. Lorraine Brown was coming in at 8:00 to train her on the switchboard.

The early morning silence that enveloped the reception area gave Adiva an eerie feeling. She soon realized that she'd arrived before anyone else.

Adiva noticed a wall with glass bookshelves built into it adjacent to the receptionist's center. She walked over to it to get a closer look. The glass shelves were adorned with numerous awards that the PPK agency had garnered over the years. Some were made of crystal while others appeared to be bronze statuettes. Adiva recognized the statuettes as ADDYs, notable awards given by the advertising industry for various creative accomplishments. Adiva had often imagined herself attending an advertising awards banquet accepting an ADDY for best copywriting on some print advertisement or a television commercial.

As her thoughts lingered on the picture perfect image in her mind, suddenly it occurred to her. This agency could be the focus of her research report for school. It was a great idea. As an employee of PPK she'd have a first-hand view of just what made this agency tick. Prophet, Priest and King would make an excellent subject matter. Adiva decided that first she'd do some background research into the early years of the agency. Then she'd highlight some of PPK's best ad campaigns. Maybe she'd even interview some of the agency's clients to get their feedback. Her journalism studies would serve her well in writing this report.

Look at me, she thought to herself. She'd gotten her foot into the door of one of the hottest advertising agencies in the country. Her parents would have been proud. Granted, she was just a receptionist, but Adiva knew in her heart that this new job was only the first rung on a ladder that she was determined to climb to greater heights.

While waiting for Lorraine to arrive, Adiva wondered about the opulent facilities of her new PPK home. Before she realized it, she found herself staring at the brass nameplate affixed to the large mahogany door of Harvard Prophet.

What kind of man was this Mr. Prophet, she wondered? As she ran her fingers across the polished wood on the door, she suddenly emitted a faint scream after being startled by a man's voice.

"What do you think you're doing?"

Adiva clasped her hand over her chest and quickly exhaled. "You scared me," she answered, immediately recognizing the man standing before her as Harvard Prophet himself. She'd only before his photograph in an issue of Advertising Age magazine. She stepped away from the door as Harvard moved hastily toward it as if he was a member of the Secret Service entrusted with protecting the President of the United States.

"I did not intend to frighten you," Harvard mumbled an apology. "But I would have thought that *you people* completed your tasks last night."

"Excuse me?"

He fumbled with the keys to unlock his door. "The *cleaning*," he replied, finally opening the door and stepping inside. "I thought that you people took care of these janitorial tasks at night," he repeated in frustration.

Adiva was shocked. She wondered how this man could even remotely presume that she was part of some nightly cleaning crew. Here she stood before him dressed in a perfectly-fitting *Donna Karan* suit, a pair of *Evan Picone* pumps, and visibly clinging from her shoulder was a *Dooney and Bourke* handbag.

She took a deep breath before speaking as she followed Harvard into his office. She was oblivious to the ritzy surroundings. "I don't mean to be rude, Mr. Prophet," Adiva began. "But I resent the fact that you don't even take the time to introduce yourself to a young lady before making erroneous assumptions about her."

Harvard Prophet turned and stared down into the flawless, fair-skinned face that was articulating to him. "Who the hell are you?" he growled.

"Adiva," she answered, staring directly into his pinched face.

He gave her a quick once-over before responding. "A *Diva* you say?" he sneered. "Well, my dear, whatever helps you sleep through the night."

Adiva tightened the reins on her tongue. "Mr. Prophet, my name *is* Adiva - *Adiva Roberts*. And I'm not part of any nightly or daily cleaning crew, thank you!"

"Well, I should hope not!" Harvard exclaimed, quickly averting his gaze away from her. "The very day that our cleaning people begin to dress like *that* will be the day I refuse to pay one red cent in rent for this office space!"

Adiva watched him as he stammered around his office. She was very disappointed to learn that Harvard Prophet was simply an idiotic stereotypical old white man.

"There you are!" came Princeton King's voice as he poked his red head into Harvard's office. "Lorraine is waiting for you up front," he informed Adiva.

"I'm sorry," Adiva apologized. "I got here early and sort of wandered around . . . "

"What the hell's going on here, Princeton?" Harvard interrupted Adiva.

Princeton glanced at Adiva and then at Harvard. "Apparently you two haven't met," he said.

"Well, um . . . "

"I know who I am and I know who you are, Princeton!" Harvard interrupted Adiva again. "Now for the last time, who the hell is this woman and what's she doing snooping around my office?"

"*Snooping*?" Adiva repeated with surprise.

"Snooping?" Princeton echoed.

"That's correct! I caught her outside my door when I arrived this morning. She appeared to be searching for a way to get inside my office!"

Princeton stared at Adiva, looking for some kind of an explanation. Adiva simply hunched her shoulders in despair. "Listen, Harvard," Princeton began as he stepped fully into the office suite. "There seem to be a slight misunderstanding. This woman is Adiva Roberts."

"I've gathered that much already," Harvard sternly stated.

"Of course. Well, Adiva is our new receptionist." Princeton went on to explain that he'd hired Adiva yesterday and that amid the flurry of activity over the CorpAir announcement, he didn't have time to put out an official memorandum. Harvard Prophet didn't mandate seeking his blessing when it came to the hiring of clerical personnel. However, he did insist on personally meeting with anyone being considered for positions within account management, media or creative.

Harvard made a quick and somewhat superficial attempt to change his demeanor. "As the head of PPK, allow me to welcome you aboard, Miss Roberts," he uttered feigningly.

"Thank you, sir," Adiva forced a smile.

The three of them stood in silence for a moment until the sound of Harvard clearing his throat interrupted the quietness. "Uh, Miss Roberts, I believe that Mr. King here mentioned that our office manager is awaiting your presence up front, did he not?"

"Oh, that's right, Adiva. Lorraine is waiting for you," Princeton chimed in.

"Well, I guess I'd better be going," Adiva said sheepishly as she headed toward the door.

"I'll check in on you later," Princeton told her. "You're going to do just fine."

Adiva nodded her head in agreement as she exited Harvard's office. There was something strange about this Mr. Prophet, she thought to herself as she walked away.

"Close the door, Princeton," Harvard instructed, pointing at his door.

Princeton quickly complied.

"Is that the best you could do?" Harvard groaned.

"I'm not sure that I know what you mean?"

"Her!" he snapped. "Why her!"

He doesn't approve of Adiva, Princeton surmised. "Sir, she's perfectly qualified for the job," Princeton attempted to defend his selection.

"I don't give a damn about her qualifications! I thought we'd already hired our fair share of minorities for this agency!"

Princeton had never heard the old man speak in such a manner. It had become apparent over the years that the advertising industry as a whole lacked sufficient minority representation in virtually every occupation. Princeton realized that PPK was by no means a model agency when it came to diversity. Their agency employed just some four ethnic minorities prior to Adiva's hiring. He'd personally vowed to do whatever he could do to recruit qualified minority talent for PPK. And it was an effort he recalled Harvard fully supporting publicly. Now, Princeton questioned the old man's sincerity.

"Harvard, I wasn't aware that we ever had a *quota* with regards to hiring minorities," Princeton said to him.

"In reality Princeton, we do not. However, in principle, we do," Harvard stated.

"Whose principle?"

"Mine! I mean, this agency's," Harvard quickly asserted.

"Well, as a fifteen-percent owner of this agency, how come I never knew about this unwritten principle?"

"Harvard threw up his hands in frustration. "You see that's the problem with you - everything's not always in black and white! We have a certain image to uphold ... a certain representation that I believe our clients expect of us. I mean, how many of our clients are African-American, Princeton?"

"Zero," Princeton quickly answered. "But, how many African-Americans purchase our clients' products and services?" he shot back.

The question apparently ruffled Harvard's feathers. He took his *Mont Blanc* and slammed it onto his desk. "That's beside the point!" he shouted. And, in a desire to eschew the subject altogether, he quickly moved to something else before Princeton had a chance to respond. "I need an update on your brainstorming session from yesterday. We've got to pull out every available resource if we're going to remain agency-of-record for CorpAir."

Princeton hesitated. He didn't want to leave this issue unresolved. Although, he realized that trying to persuade Harvard Prophet to change his view on the matter would be futile at this point. Thus, he chose to go along with Harvard's creative avoidance for now and focus attention on a much bigger crisis. He explained to Harvard that the brainstorming session yesterday had yielded little results. No one on the creative team could come up with any unique angles to present to their largest client. Princeton figured that the initial shock of the announced review on his team was yet to wear off.

Harvard told him to keep the sessions going. "Spend the night here if you have to!" he blared.

The short list of contenders for the CorpAir account had been finalized late yesterday. It was without a doubt that this review was not going to drag on for several months. Harvard reiterated to Princeton that they needed to be prepared to make initial presentations in less than thirty days.

Harvard had met privately yesterday evening with Douglas Sheldon in hopes of convincing him to scratch the entire review process. But Douglas Sheldon could not be persuaded. He told Harvard that it was time to shake things up a bit. To see what else was out there. And before the meeting ended, Douglas assured Harvard that whatever happened from the review, that he must remain open-minded and that he must not take it personally. However, the well-rehearsed advice had fallen upon deaf ears. The potential loss of a $50 million account was not the sort of thing a man could chalk up to business as usual. Harvard Prophet believed that he'd earned the right to keep and grow his $50 million account. And if someone - anyone - tried to take it away from him he'd have no choice but to view it as a personal attack against everything that he'd spent his life building. And when the very essence of a man was under attack, such a man had to determine whether or not he was going to fight back.

Harvard Prophet was a fighter. And now that the battle cry had been sounded, he realized that he was preparing to wage war like it had never been waged before.

CHAPTER EIGHT

BY THE END OF THE WEEK, THE INITIAL fracas concerning the CorpAir review had subsided somewhat. And it seemed as though a dark cloud had settled over the entire PPK staff. Somber faces of uncertainty replaced their usual late afternoon jesting and cajoling. Management personnel trampled in and out of Harvard Prophet's office throughout the week.

The agency's anniversary celebration that was held Monday night at the Marriott Marquis in downtown Atlanta had gone quite well - all things considered. While there were pockets of conversation regarding the CorpAir review, the evening focused primarily on the success of Prophet, Priest & King and its superlative leader.

The creative department, which was led by Princeton King, had been conducting brainstorming sessions behind the glass walls of the agency's auxiliary conference room. And Duke Priest spent much of the week trying to allay the concerns of PPK's other clients. The loss of an account the size of CorpAir could easily open the door for other client defections. And although the fate of the $50 million account was yet to be decided upon, implementing a plan for possible damage control had become paramount.

Duke Priest sat at his desk laboriously massaging his temples. His index fingers were pressed firmly against both sides of his forehead. He was attempting to rid himself of an excruciating headache. He could hardly wait until four o'clock this afternoon when he was scheduled to meet with his psychiatrist.

Duke had gone through a traumatic divorce five years ago. On the one-year anniversary since his divorce he nearly killed himself by taking an overdose of painkillers. The emotional scars that were left behind from his divorce could no longer be suppressed. Quite regularly now he struggled with what he believed to be bouts of depression.

Since he began meeting with Dr. Hetzler on Friday afternoons for the past year, he began to allow himself to finally face his demons. No one at PPK knew that he was seeing a psychiatrist, except Princeton. Duke had insisted on having his sessions with the doctor scheduled on Fridays since he almost always left the office by three o'clock on Fridays. This, he hoped, would alleviate the need to take time off for repeated doctor visits. And the Friday afternoon sessions would also squelch any suspicion of his whereabouts from his counterparts.

Duke slowly peeled the slightly brown banana that he retrieved from his center desk drawer and began chomping away at it. He'd harbored an insatiable appetite for the fruit ever since he was a kid.

Growing up under the guidance of a single parent, there was very little money to splurge on such delights as bananas. Duke's father had walked out on the family when he just six years old. And since Duke couldn't afford to buy the fruit he enjoyed so much, he would steal bananas from a small corner grocery store. From age eight until he was sixteen, he stole at least one banana every day from Mr. Cohen's Neighborhood Market. He figured that he must have stolen over 3,000 bananas during his childhood. He'd promised himself that one-day he would go back to his old neighborhood and repay every penny to Mr. Cohen for the bananas. But by the time Duke graduated from college, Mr. Cohen's Neighborhood Market had gone out of business – a victim of hideous and repeated robberies. Duke could never quite absolve the guilt from his conscience. He blamed himself for having contributed to the demise of what had become a neighborhood icon.

Duke checked his watch. It was 2:33. The day was almost over. He threw the banana peel into his wastebasket and then made a mental note to pick up another bunch on his way in to work on Monday.

He began to straighten the papers that were scattered about his desk, stuffing some into his attaché case. He flipped the light switch to turn off the lights. As he began to lock his door, he could see that Princeton was still in his office two doors down.

"Why are you still here?" Duke asked, stopping in front of Princeton's doorway. Princeton generally left the office by noon on Fridays.

"Just tying up some loose ends," Princeton replied.

Actually, he was waiting for some earlier beers to wear off before he attempted to drive home.

"I see. Well, have a good weekend," Duke waved to him in a military salute style.

"Hey listen, Duke," Princeton called to him.

Duke reappeared in the doorway.

"What's your honest take on this CorpAir review?"

Duke let out a deep sigh. "To be honest, Princeton, I really don't know. Personally, I want to believe that CorpAir is just tugging at our chain. It wouldn't be the first time."

Princeton joined Duke in the doorway of his office. "It seems to be the prevailing trend," Princeton stated.

Duke leaned his left shoulder against Princeton's office door and began to scratch his head. "Yeah, I suppose you're right. I mean *Toyzuki* just yanked their $40 million automotive account from the grasp of *Arrington and Partners.*"

Princeton shook his head. "This business just keeps getting crazier. Was it a New York shop that picked up the account?" Princeton was curious.

"Surprisingly, no. They gave the account to *Coleman Eilers* out of Dallas," Duke explained. "In fact they're a wholly-owned subsidiary of the *Gentsu Group*, which, by-the-way, already handles Toyzuki in Japan."

Princeton chuckled. "An apparent shoo-in," he quipped. "Boy, it must have been a devastating blow to Arrington."

Duke let his attaché case drop to the floor beside him. "Obviously so – especially since they're also in the middle of trying to defend another $30 million loss from the California Department of Energy Resources."

"Are you serious?"

"Of course. When it rains it pours. And the irony is how similar our situations are."

"Meaning?"

"Well, first, Arrington bills around $120 million a year. They've maintained Toyzuki on their roster for about a decade, and get this—" Duke paused for emphasis. "The reason given for the Toyzuki loss had nothing to do with the agency's management of the account . . . "

"Let me guess," Princeton interrupted. "There was a *change* in key personnel!"

"You got it," confirmed Duke. "Toyzuki had a reshuffling in top executives. And as you and I know, when that happens the current agency is pretty much history."

"Well, I don't think that any agency is immune," Princeton said. "Although there was a time when I actually believed that we were."

"We've just been lucky," Duke told him. "And whether or not our luck is about to run out remains to be seen."

Princeton began stroking his chin. "Let's just hope that Harvey boy is getting all worked up over nothing - even though I do enjoy watching him squirm."

Duke chuckled. "Yeah, you're right."

"Maybe this review will take his mind off acquiring our thirty-percent," Princeton said in a whisper.

"Well, he may be closer to getting my fifteen-percent more than he realizes," Duke remarked.

"You're kidding me?"

"Unfortunately, I'm not."

Duke had been discussing his lack of interest in the agency lately with Dr. Hetzler.

"Duke, I'd appreciate it if you talk to me first before selling your interest to the old man."

"I'll keep that in mind."

The two men stood in silence momentarily. "I guess I'd better get back to mulling over new ideas that will help us save CorpAir," Princeton stated, breaking the silence.

"CorpAir could go to hell for all I care," Duke said emphatically. "But don't tell Harvard I said that!" he quickly added.

They both laughed.

"Look at this way, Duke. If we lose the account we lose it. Now I realize that it would be a fifty-million dollar loss, but hey - life goes on."

"Yeah, I guess you're right. But I wouldn't try telling that to old man Harvey." Duke remarked, solemnly.

◊◊◊◊◊◊◊

Harvard Prophet found himself cursing into his telephone again. It was something that he'd been doing all week. This time, however, it wasn't to overly ambitious reporters. "Listen to me, dammit! I've been patient long enough! I don't give a damn what you have to do, but I want you to make this thing happen, understand?"

"I can't guarantee it," the voice on the other end answered.

"Is it more money you want? Is that it?"

"No, no. Of course not, Harvard. The money has been more than generous. It's just that we're dealing with a very delicate situation."

"I'm not paying you for delicacy, dammit! Just make sure that this transaction takes place soon!" Harvard slammed the telephone receiver down. He could feel his blood pressure boiling.

There was a soft knock at his door.

"Go home!" Harvard snarled.

The door opened anyway. It was Seymour Boudreau, the thirty-two year-old black Frenchman and vice president of media.

"What are you still doing hanging around, Seymour?" Harvard asked, his voice calmer.

Seymour approached Harvard's desk. "I just wanted to drop this off to you," he answered, handing Harvard a new CD.

"What's this?"

"It's a collection of her greatest hits," Seymour explained.

Harvard stared vacuously at the CD. Most of the agency's staff knew how much he enjoyed listening to Aretha Franklin's tunes from the 1960's. During those rare moments when he was in a good mood they would all know it because Aretha Franklin's soulful voice could be heard belching from Harvard's CD player that was maintained in his office.

"Thank you, Seymour."

"My pleasure, sir. In light of this week's circumstances, I thought it would be a splendid respite."

"Perhaps it will. Again, thank you. It was a very noble gesture."

After Seymour had left his office, Harvard began to unwrap the tightly secured plastic that was protecting the CD. When he finally succeeded at opening it, he popped it into his CD player.

As Aretha's soothing voice began to ooze from the speakers, he closed his eyes and rested his head back against his leather chair. He knew Aretha would make him feel better. He used the remote to increase the music's volume. Then he quietly allowed the *Queen of Soul* to take him away from this helluva week that he'd been put through.

CHAPTER NINE

THE OFFICES OF HETZLER PSYCHIATRIC Care, P.C. were located in a small suite on the sixth floor of an aging office tower in the Sandy Springs suburb of Atlanta. Fifty-four year-old Philip James Hetzler, M.D. ran the practice alone. His staff of four assistants had been reduced to only one. And her hours were limited to part-time.

Dr. Hetzler stood about five-feet-nine. He mainly draped his sinewy frame in tan slacks, a short-sleeved Polo shirt and a navy blue sport jacket. His thick, black framed eyeglasses were unable to shield the mirthful crinkles surrounding his eyes. And when he spoke he had a bad habit of clearing his throat many times as he attempted to correct his tremulous voice.

The number of patients making appointments to see Dr. Hetzler had also been reduced dramatically. Two years ago he was so over-booked that he considered bringing aboard another doctor to help him manage the practice. But now, he could barely afford to pay himself - least of all keep his doors opened.

He knew that treating patients is what he was destined to do with his life. He was a board certified psychiatrist with over twenty-seven years of experience. And the last fifteen years have been spent in his personal practice.

Duke Priest was visibly relaxed as he was lying on the firm, black leather sofa in Dr. Hetzler's office. Duke tried to escape the demands and pressures of the ad agency as he listened to *Mozart's Piano Concerto Number 26* playing melodiously throughout the modest office. Dr. Hetzler was discussing Duke's claim that he was having difficulty getting over his moods of depression.

"Simply put, I'm fed up with the agency," Duke explained. "I mean I literally hate the place."

"Why do you suppose that is?" Dr. Hetzler questioned, as he jotted down notes on a large white notepad.

Duke hunched his shoulders. "I don't know."

"Duke, as I'm sure you'll recall when we started these sessions it was to help you to come to terms with the demise of your marriage. However, I have observed over the past several weeks that our discussions have begun to center primarily on your discontentment with your role at the ad agency."

Duke lay quietly on the sofa and listened. He'd never really paid much attention to their specific discussions each week. Just being in the doctor's office was a refuge for him. They could have discussed nuclear disarmament or the theory of relativity for all he cared. Duke Priest just wanted an escape from the toilsome tasks of the ad agency business. He was sick of futile strategizing. He was tired of appeasing the egos of marketing vp's. Basically, Duke no longer wanted to kiss the butts of clients who threaten to take their multi-million dollar accounts elsewhere.

"My role at the agency has taken its toll on me, Phil," Duke spoke in a hushed tone. He paused before he continued. "You know, it was the agency that caused the problems in my marriage. Sylvia warned me many times about all the hours I was spending at PPK. But of course, I never listened to her."

Dr. Hetzler scribbled more notes.

"After all," Duke continued. "What did she know?" he asked rhetorically. "What did she know?" he repeated, almost in a whisper.

"Duke, it's been five years since your divorce," Dr. Hetzler interjected. "Are you still experiencing some emotional pain as a result of the divorce?"

A slight chuckle managed to escape from Duke's pursed lips. "If you're asking me am I over my ex-wife, Phil, the answer should be obvious," he answered. "Who knows - maybe I never will be."

"Then tell me . . . how do you know if you're depressed over losing your marriage or if it's due to your dissatisfaction with your career?"

"Isn't that's why I'm paying you, Phil?"

Dr. Hetzler found himself squirming in his chair, his face beginning to flush as well. "Yes, of course. But if I may elaborate, Duke, what I'm trying to ascertain is your own feelings or reasons as to why you believe you're depressed . . ."

Duke closed his eyes as he shifted his posture on the sofa. For the moment he chose to ignore the doctor's voice speaking to him. He chose instead to allow his mind and soul to become consumed by the magic of Mozart. The man's music was totally mesmerizing and incredibly soothing.

Next to his insatiable appetite for bananas, Duke had a prodigious love for classical music. He and Sylvia became immediate supporters of the Atlanta Symphony upon their arrival to the city over a decade ago. Princeton had always chided him about it. The idea of a young man in his twenties being so enthralled by the symphony seemed out of the ordinary, Princeton once remarked. But little did Princeton know, Duke had been a champion for the classics all of his life. Throughout high school he participated in the school band - excelling quite well on the violin. And it was the school band where he'd met Sylvia. He remembered how perfect her lips were for playing the flute. He missed her dearly.

Since their divorce he's had very little contact with her. They never had any children so there was no reason to keep the communication lines open. Duke assumed that she's moved on with her life. Married by now, he presumed. Maybe even a child or two. A stable and loving family. It was what she always talked about. It was what he was unable to provide.

"Excuse me, Duke?" Dr. Hetzler's voice interrupted his brief journey down memory lane.

"Oh, I'm awake, Phil," Duke joked. "Just resting my eyes, that's all."

"Well, would you like to continue our discussion?" Dr. Hetzler asked.

Duke sat up on the sofa. "Actually, Phil, I think that if you were to simply prescribe some medication for these mood swings, I can get out of your hair for awhile."

"Medication?"

"Sure! I think its time I got a bit of that *wonder drug* I've been hearing so much about in my system!"

Dr. Hetzler placed his notepad and pencil down onto his desk. He removed his eyeglasses and began, "Look, Duke. Your overall emotional well being is of the utmost importance to me. However, to be quite frank with you, I'm not in the habit of dispensing medications to my patients until I'm absolutely certain that such is absolutely necessary."

"Well, I'm telling you that it is necessary," Duke stated strongly. "And I believe that the patient is always right!"

"Let's not confuse my profession with your line of work, Duke," Dr. Hetzler politely reprimanded. "For your business *the customer is always right* – but it doesn't necessarily work that way in the medical profession – at least not in my practice anyway."

"So what are you saying, Doc? That my opinion is no good?"

"Of course not. Now listen, I'm simply asking that you allow me to first determine if you are what we refer to as being *clinically depressed,* or if you're simply experiencing some *down-in-the-dumps* episodes, okay?"

Duke lay down on the sofa again, resting his folded hands on top of his protruding stomach. "I hate feeling like this all the time," he spoke, looking up towards the ceiling. "If *Prozac* will do the trick, then that's what I want!"

Dr. Hetzler stood from his chair and walked to the other side of his desk and sat down in one of his winged-back chairs that was positioned directly across from the sofa where Duke lay.

"Over seventeen million Americans suffer clinical depression at any given time," he started explaining. "You may very well be among that group, Duke. However, another fifteen million or so Americans simply experience mild symptoms of just being *down-in-the-dumps.* Now, if you're in the latter, Duke, then *Prozac, Zoloft* or *Paxil* or any one of the other *SSRIs* out there isn't the answer."

"I don't know anything about *SSIs* or *So-Soft,*" Duke stated, unable to remember the exact terminology just used by the doctor. "I've just heard that *Prozac* works for people who are depressed."

"It's called Zoloft with a 'Z'," Dr. Hetzler corrected him. "And it is an *SSRI* just like *Prozac, Paxil* and some others. And *SSRI* simply stands for *selective serotonin reuptake inhibitors* - also known as antidepressants."

"Fine. Prescribe for me an antidepressant," Duke told him.

Dr. Hetzler paused before responding. "Duke, I am not doubting your condition. In fact, for the record, based on the experiences that you've shared having lasted for more than two weeks, my initial diagnosis would be that you are indeed perhaps suffering clinical depression."

"Okay. Now that we agree, Phil, can you just write the prescription so that I can get out of here and start feeling better?"

Dr. Hetzler began to clear his throat. "What I prefer is that we try the psychotherapy approach for the next few sessions and then see what happens . . . "

"Psychotherapy?"

"Yes. It is basically what you and I have been doing for months now - discussing the events taking place in your life, your feelings, etc."

"So then, since we've already been doing this psychotherapy thing for months, what's the point in doing it some more? It obviously hasn't worked!"

"Because we have focused primarily on you overcoming the demise of your marriage. And you've just recently shared with me your persistent down moods, your loss of energy, and your loss of interest in your career. Now, these are all certainly signs of depression. However, I simply want to be sure that you're not just reacting to a *depressive situation.*"

"When you say a few more sessions, Phil, what are we talking about – a couple of weeks? A month? What?"

"Well, that all depends upon the results of each psychotherapy session. But Duke, let me assure you that if at any time during the psychotherapy phase it becomes apparent to me that an antidepressant will help, then I will get you started on Zoloft."

"I want Prozac."

Dr. Hetzler emitted a faint sigh. "I generally prescribe Zoloft to my patients. But we can discuss the appropriate brand at the appropriate time."

"Fine."

Dr. Hetzler retreated back to his chair behind his desk. "I wish to ask you a hypothetical question?" he said to Duke, switching subject matter. "Have you ever given any thought to simply relinquishing your role at the ad agency?"

Duke pondered the question for a moment. Of course, he'd given thought to it numerous times. But what else was he supposed to do? "That's easier said than done, Phil. I'm a partner in the agency. I have certain fiduciary responsibilities."

"I understand," Dr. Hetzler acknowledged. "However, do you really believe that PPK won't be able to function in your absence?"

Duke realized that the agency could function quite nicely without him. Old man Harvard would be one step closer to gaining his one-hundred-percent control. The question was whether or not Duke Priest could function without the agency. Advertising was his life. And as much as he deplored it right now, he wouldn't know how to do anything else. He was thirty-nine years old. Too young to retire. He didn't play golf. A social life of any kind was practically non-existent. What kind of a future awaited him if he didn't have PPK to occupy his time and consume what little energy he had remaining?

"To be really honest with you, Phil, I have entertained that thought on numerous occasions," he admitted solemnly.

"Then why not do it!" Dr. Hetzler yelled, oblivious to his own raised tone of voice. "Owning this agency has been a noose around your neck, Duke! Cut the rope! You've got to cut the damn rope!"

Dr. Hetzler quickly realized how adamant he'd become. He regained his composure. "I'm sorry. I didn't mean to get all worked up over this. It's just that . . . well, I see what owning this agency is doing to you – a dear patient of mine. Now, I'm not saying that you'd have to stop working at PPK. But I do believe, however, that if you were to relinquished your *ownership* stake in the agency, you would perhaps free yourself from the mental and emotional strains that seem to have encumbered you."

Duke had never considered the fact that if he simply gave up his partnership status that he could still work for the agency. "I need to think about this awhile," Duke told him.

"Certainly. But do not procrastinate, Duke. The sooner we get you over this hurdle the sooner we can begin determining the level of your depression - if any at all."

The two of them went on to discuss the improvement Duke was making in coping with his divorce. Dr. Hetzler encouraged him to begin dating. Duke wasn't ready to take that step.

After Duke had left the doctor's office, Dr. Hetzler quickly placed a phone call. The voice that answered wasn't the one that he was expecting. "With whom am I speaking?" Dr. Hetzler asked.

"*Whom* do you want to speak with?"

"Harvard Prophet, please."

"He is not available. I'm his daughter, may I help you or take a message?"

"No. I will try and reach him later."

"May I tell my father who called?"

Click.

Dr. Hetzler scanned the columns of his personal telephone directory and found Harvard's cell phone number. He dialed it. Harvard answered on the second ring.

"Harvard, it's me, Philip."

"Good news I hope, Phil?"

"We're almost there. I believe he's going to do it."

"What do you mean you *believe*?"

"Harvard, he is ready to cash in his chips. He just wants a little time to come to terms with the decision."

Harvard mumbled obscenities under his breath. "I've waited this long, I suppose a little more time won't hurt. But I'm warning you Phil, it sure as hell better happen soon! I have paid you quite handsomely these past few months. I want a completed transaction!"

Dr. Hetzler bristled at Harvard's demand. "And I have risked my professional career over this lousy transaction!" he charged.

"Oh I don't give a damn about your professional career! Have you taken a peek at your bank statement recently? You couldn't bill enough hours to make the amount of money that I've paid you in six months!" Harvard reminded him in no uncertain terms. "You know as well as I do that if I hadn't come along when I did, your so-called *professional career* would have been as good as dead. So don't you dare try and lecture me, Phil Hetzler! Just give me the return on my investment that I'm expecting – nothing less!"

Click.

Dr. Hetzler held the phone in his hand for a few seconds before finally placing it back onto the receiver. Money or no money, he felt like a dejected man. He couldn't believe that he'd compromised his professional ethics. When Harvard Prophet approached him six months ago after he'd learned that Duke was one of his patients, he should have refused his offer. But at the time, the request that Harvard made seemed so simple, so harmless. After all, it was becoming clear that Duke had lost interest in the agency. What harm could have been done in persuading him to sell his minority stake in the agency? The guilt consuming him was becoming almost unbearable. He realized that he was in too deep to turn back now.

Sure, he'd provide Harvard Prophet with his *completed transaction*. He'd take the final payment of $150,000 in cash. In return, he also realized that his professional career would essentially be over. To continue to practice psychiatric counseling after having sold his morals and his ethics would be beyond hypocritical. He knew that no amount of money in the world could compensate for what he'd done. He felt as though he'd come to the brink of utter ruin. It was only a matter of time now before his downfall. The professional community would abhor him. The mere mention of his name would become repulsive. He wondered how politicians did it so easily and were still able to live with themselves. He also knew that he could never provide a plausible explanation to his wife and three grown children about his indefensible actions. Their respect and trust in him would be totally destroyed.

Perhaps the cliché was true – everything did have its price. And for Philip James Hetzler, M.D., the egomaniacal Harvard Prophet was quickly marking down his price tag.

CHAPTER TEN

THE BRONZE PEACH WAS A BLACK-OWNED and operated upscale restaurant and jazz club that was located in the heart of Atlanta's ritzy Buckhead section of town. The two-story brick and glass structure was competitively situated at the intersection of Peachtree and Pharr Roads. Valet parking was provided as a customer amenity.

As patrons entered through the double doors, which were shaped into a curvaceous peach and constructed of bronze, they were welcomed by a young and attractive black female hostess who's pleasantries gave a novel meaning to the phrase 'service with a smile'. Frequent visitors to The Bronze Peach included many of Atlanta's rising professionals, popular athletes and entertainment celebrities.

Although the conservative décor of The Bronze Peach was warm and inviting, Adiva Roberts felt uncomfortable as she sat alone at a small table near the three-feet high stage where her boyfriend, Soupa Mann, was due to perform at any moment.

This was Adiva's first time being in The Bronze Peach. It wasn't the type of establishment she preferred to frequent. She wasn't the party type and she didn't drink alcohol - both of which were a big part of Soupa Mann's repertoire.

She forced herself to come to The Bronze Peach on this Saturday evening because it was Soupa Mann's first opportunity to sing here, although he was a regular patron of the place.

Adiva and Soupa Mann have been dating for two years. She would like to see their relationship go farther, but she wasn't so sure if Soupa Mann felt the same way. She figured that his divorce, after ten years of marriage, probably made him tread more cautiously where relationships were concerned.

Soupa Mann didn't get a chance to visit his twelve year-old son as much as he would like since the boy lived in California with his mother. Adiva questioned Soupa Mann once about where things stood between him and his ex-wife. He tried to assure her that there was no opening in his life for reconciliation, even though his ex-wife had an ardent interest in finding one.

Adiva found herself feeling skeptical. She wanted to believe him, but the ex-wife factor plus a child together usually spelled trouble. At least Granny Rae was determined to get her to see it that way.

Adiva picked up her half-full glass of Diet Coke and began to slowly stir the square chunks of ice inside the glass with her index finger. A mist had formed around the outside of the glass. She wiped away part of the mist with her thumb and stared into the side of the glass. The dark fizzling liquid precluded her from seeing her reflection. She set the glass back down onto the table without taking a sip.

Adiva glanced at her watch. It was almost seven-thirty. Soupa Mann was supposed to be out on the stage at seven. She'd been sitting in The Bronze Peach for an hour and a half now.

She was oblivious to the roar of laughter and chatter as the place began to quickly fill up with ready-to-party patrons. She wondered just how many of these people would be in worship service tomorrow morning. It was her religious conviction and commitment that caused her to feel even more uncomfortable. Soupa Mann would owe her big time for this sacrifice. And she knew just what he would have to do to settle his debt - have his singing butt in church tomorrow with her - singing hymns to the Lord.

◈◈◈◈◈◈◈

It was almost nine-o'clock when Soupa Mann finished his one-hour of entertainment with a rousing rendition of James Ingram's tune *Just Once.* The women in the crowd, those who had obviously had more than one *Long Island Iced Tea,* became ghetto-wild. There was more screaming and yelling inside The Bronze Peach than inside a hospital nursery full of unfed newborns.

Soupa Mann was easily soaking it all in as he sauntered his iron-muscled frame off the stage and carefully negotiated his way towards Adiva. His charismatic smile flashed brighter than headlights on a dark highway at every woman shouting out his name as he passed by their table.

When he finally reached the table where Adiva was seated, he gave her a coquettish grin before planting a kiss on her lips. "Okay, baby. What's the *verdict*?" he asked, taking a seat across from her.

"You should be able to tell based on all these screaming *jurors*," she chided.

"Aw, c'mon baby. You know I don't care nothing 'bout what they think. It's your opinion that matters to me," he told her. "Now, be honest - what did you think of my performance tonight?"

Adiva lifted her now empty glass of Diet Coke and attempted to drain another sip. Instead, she only felt the cold leftover ice bumping against her top lip. She placed the glass back onto the table. "Well, I've heard better," she answered

His grin dissipated. "You've heard better?" he repeated, less enthusiasm in his voice.

"Yes. I mean, I had to fight myself to keep from booing you off the stage," she said, trying to maintain a straight face.

"Why didn't you?"

"Because you looked and sounded so pitiful that I just couldn't do that to a brother."

"Well thank you for all your support!" he nearly shouted at her.

"You're welcome," she continued the charade. "It was the least I could do," she added, sarcastically.

"I can't believe you would be that cold," he said solemnly.

"You asked me to be honest," Adiva protested.

"Yeah, I know. But I was hoping for some *constructive* criticism."

Adiva burst into laughter. "Gotcha!" she screamed.

Soupa Mann looked relieved. "Naw, I knew you were lying the whole time," he retorted, trying to save face.

"Yeah, right!"

The couple joked some more as Soupa Mann nibbled on Adiva's basket of half-eaten fries.

"I need to be going," Adiva told him, noticing the time.

"Why the rush, baby? We've still got more celebrating to do," he said, referring to his intention on celebrating her new job this week.

Adiva shook her head. "No, I really should be going. I don't feel comfortable staying out late with my grandmother all by herself."

"Your grandmamma is probably asleep by now."

"Don't bet on it. She's not going to sleep until I walk through the door safe and sound. Besides, I have to get up early for church in the morning."

Soupa Mann relented. He realized how many promises he'd made to attend church with her and he hadn't fulfilled any of them. "Yeah, I guess you're right," he was eager to agree. "I'll walk you to your car." He stood from his chair.

"Not so fast," she stopped him.

Oh boy, here it comes. "Um, what's the problem?"

"There's not a problem. It's just that in return for me sacrificing my morals to come into this place, I expect you to be joining me in church tomorrow morning," she said matter-of-factly.

"Aw now, baby. You know I plan to visit your church soon . . . "

"It's *The Lord's Church,*" she interrupted him. "Not mine."

"How 'bout I come next Sunday – I don't have anything scheduled for next weekend."

"What do you have scheduled for tomorrow, Soupa Mann?"

He fiddled with his chin. "Well, you know . . . I'm gonna hang around here for awhile and so I'll need tomorrow to rest up before I go to work on Monday."

"If you were to leave now, with me, you'll have plenty of time to rest up tonight for our nine-o'clock worship service in the morning. And we'll be out before noon, so you'll then have the remainder of the day to rest before Monday."

She wasn't going to let up. "All right, you win," he surrendered. "I'll go to church with you tomorrow."

Adiva was surprised that he gave in so quickly. She shot him a dubious glance. "Are you for real?"

"Hey baby, I said I would go."

"Need I remind you that you've been promising *'to go'* for the past year."

He quickly absorbed the guilt she threw at him and just as quickly he brushed it aside. "Well, tomorrow the promise will be fulfilled," he assured her.

Adiva was elated. Finally! He was going to take an interest in the Lord and maybe, just maybe experience the spiritual joy, renewal and encouragement from Brother Blake's sermons that she and Granny Rae experienced every Sunday.

She reached across the table and took hold of his right hand with her left hand and gave it a gentle squeeze. "Thank you, Soupa Mann."

He squeezed her hand as well as he gave her an affected smile. Unbeknownst to Adiva Roberts, Soupa Mann's other hand lay beneath the table upon his knee with his fingers tightly crossed.

Forgive me, Jesus, he thought to himself.

The Lord's Church was a non-denominational congregation of about five hundred members from different racial backgrounds - African-American, White and Asian. Their recently constructed building, located in Roswell just north of Atlanta, did not resemble a traditional church building. The two-story building, with a grayish stucco exterior, was absent stained glass windows. Its interior was equally conservative, lined with cushiony pews throughout the first floor auditorium and the balcony area.

The congregation's minister was a black sixty year-old retired Georgia Tech professor and widower named Henry Blake.

The men in the congregation were greeted as brothers by their last name, and the women were greeted as sisters by their last name. After all, the bible taught that *'we were all brothers and sisters in Christ'*.

Brother Blake was small in stature. But his thunderous voice easily commanded attention. Preaching the word of God meant everything to him. He had a genuine love and concern for others. And not only would he be willing to give the shirt off his back to anyone who needed it – he was also the sort of man who'd throw in a jacket and tie to go along.

Adiva stood quietly in the front lobby of the church building anxiously waiting for Soupa Mann. The worship service began at nine a.m. It was now 8:55. Nervously, she watched as scores of latecomers sped into the parking lot. She didn't care if Soupa Mann was one of them. She prayed that he was one of them. But there was no sign of his burgundy Jeep Cherokee pulling into one of the many *visitors'* parking spots.

Every minute or so Granny Rae would turn her head around from inside the auditorium and motion with her hand for Adiva to come and sit down. When Adiva had told her grandmother last night that Soupa Mann had decided to come to church with them, Granny Rae admonished her not to hold her breath. Adiva wanted to prove her grandmother wrong. She desperately needed to prove her wrong.

It was now nine-fifteen and the congregation was singing their fourth song before Brother Blake would begin to preach. Adiva continued to stare hopelessly through the windows silently praying that Soupa Mann hadn't broken his promise; that he was just running late. The man was driving all the way from College Park on the other side of town.

"Excuse me, Sister Roberts," came the voice from one of the ushers.

Adiva turned from the window. "Good morning, Brother Smith."

" Morning Sister Roberts - are you expecting a visitor?"

"Um, yes," she stammered. "He should have been here by now."

"Well, if you like, I'll keep an eye out for him and when he arrives I'll be happy to escort him to where you're sitting," he offered.

Adiva hesitated. She realized that she should be inside with Granny Rae. "Thank you. That's probably a good idea."

"That way you won't have to miss any part of the worship service," Brother Smith explained.

Adiva agreed with him. But before going inside the auditorium she gave the usher a description of Soupa Mann. "He's about five-feet-nine with broad shoulders," she began. "He'll probably be wearing a black blazer and a dress shirt without a tie." She knew this because Soupa Mann hated ties.

The usher listened attentively, occasionally nodding his head in agreement.

Adiva continued to rattle off Soupa Mann's physical attributes as if she was entering him in a *Mr. Universe* contest. "Oh yes, he has a light brown complexion and black curly hair that's cut into a fade . . ."

"What's his name?" Brother Smith interrupted.

That would be helpful. "Oh, I'm sorry," Adiva apologized sheepishly. "His name is Soupa Mann."

"*Superman*?" Brother Smith repeated, surprised.

Adiva quickly decided to simply spelled it out. "Soupa - S-O-U-P-A. Last name Mann - M-A-N-N." Then she offered a polite thank you, shook his hand and hurried inside the auditorium before the usher could comment any further about the name.

Adiva was able to participate in the final song. When she sat down again next to Granny Rae, absent Soupa Mann, Granny Rae cut her eyes in an *'I told you so'* manner. Adiva found the silent remark to be undeniably true.

"Brothers and Sisters," began Brother Blake, as he stepped up to the wooden podium. "Let us thank the Lord for his matchless grace! And his marvelous mercy!"

A chorus of *AMEN* erupted throughout the auditorium.

"It is indeed a privilege that we are all gathered together this morning to worship the Lord God Almighty! And to praise his Holy Name!"

AMEN! AMEN! AMEN!

"Now, let me have your undivided attention, Brothers and Sisters in Christ. Because as sure as the Lord reign up in Heaven, there is a message on my heart this morning . . ."

All right now!

" . . . It may very well be that I will step on some toes with my sermon this morning. But I want y'all to know that if I do, it's not because I'm mad at ya, but because I love ya!"

Preach Brother Blake!

"Brothers and Sisters, there is an *enemy* out there. And this enemy is against any and everything that the children of God stand for. This enemy will not rest until he has taken complete control of your life! This enemy will stop at nothing to sift you like wheat until he has devoured your very soul!"

AMEN! AMEN! AMEN!

"Now, some of you are beginning to look around the auditorium. You're already trying to identify this enemy. But I'm here to tell you that the enemy is not your husband! The enemy is not your wife! The enemy is not your children! The enemy is not your best friend! The enemy is not your mother-in-law! The enemy is not your boss at work!"

Hallelujah! AMEN! Preach On!

"Brothers and Sisters, the enemy we all need to identify this morning is Satan! That old devil himself!"

Praise the Lord!

"Wait a minute, now! Let's not get carried away in our righteousness. You see Satan is not alone down here!"

Uh Oh!

"Let me say it again for those up in the balcony – *Satan is not alone down here!*"

Brother Blake retrieved his handkerchief from his hip pocket and cleared the perspiration from his face. The congregation was clinging to his every word.

"Guess who's keeping Satan company?"

The auditorium grew overwhelmingly silent.

"Well, I'm gonna tell y'all who . . . " He cleared away more perspiration with his handkerchief. "It's your husband, it's your wife, it's your children, it's your best friend, it's your mother-in-law, and it's your boss at work!"

AMEN! Preach On!

"This brings me to the title of today's sermon. Brothers and Sisters I want to speak about *Creeping With The Enemy!*"

A thunderous applause erupted and shouts of *Amen* resounded throughout the auditorium.

The worship services and bible classes ended around eleven-thirty on that Sunday morning. Soupa Mann never showed up.

Adiva remained silent during their drive home from church. She simply listened to Granny Rae reiterate Brother Blake's sermon, as she did every Sunday on their way home from church. Granny Rae would add things that she thought Brother Blake should have said, and she would omit things that she felt shouldn't have been said. Adiva thought it best and polite to indulge her eighty-three year-old grandmother.

It had been another good sermon. *Creeping With The Enemy.* Adiva pondered the sermon's topic some more as she guided the car into their driveway. Brother Blake had used as a reference the scripture in *2 Corinthians 6:14 – 'Do not be yoked together with unbelievers . . .'*

She needed to meditate on this.

It was obvious that Brother Blake had definitely stepped on a lot of toes with this morning's sermon. And considering that her feet were beginning to ache, she realized that hers were no exception.

CHAPTER ELEVEN

THE TWO OF THEM HAD ARRANGED A 3:30 a.m. Monday meeting at an all night coffee house and diner just off Interstate-75, south of Atlanta. The place was practically empty. And judging by the appearance of *The Brew Joint,* it wasn't hard to figure out why it was nearly empty.

The hand-made menu was difficult to decipher because several items on it had been crossed out, written in with a pen, and then crossed out again. However, more than just coffee was served. *The Brew Joint* also served breakfast, lunch and dinner.

The two of them had neither a desire nor any intentions of actually eating in this debilitating hole-in-the-wall. And little did they know, *The Brew Joint* was only one more citation away from being closed down by the Public Health Department.

It was a muggy June morning. A large thermometer hanging on the front door of the place was already registering eighty-one degrees. Summers in Atlanta could be brutal. And today would be no exception. Yet, they both ordered a cup of hot decaf.

There were only four small windows inside *The Brew Joint*. The three windows facing the front of the establishment were stuck and therefore closed, while the fourth window was secluded back in the kitchen area. The place did not have an air conditioning system.

The two waitresses unfortunate enough to be working this shift lounged at the counter and chatted while smoking their cigarettes. And since they had no customers clamoring for their attention, they appeared to be amusing one another by blowing enough smoke into the air that it almost made it impossible to even read the dingy menu.

The two men attempted to keep their voices at a whisper as they discussed their *business.* A radio could be heard whimpering country tunes from the kitchen, where a lone, somewhat overweight, white man clad in a dirty-looking white T-shirt was doing the cooking. A ceiling fan, which was missing three of its five fans, twirled slowly above their heads. The creaking sound that it made with each rotation was becoming more annoying by the minute.

One of the waitresses, a middle-aged woman with scraggly blonde hair and enough make-up to put *Tammy Faye Baker* to shame, set the cups of coffee in front of them. The force of her efforts caused some of the steaming black liquid to spill over onto the table. She neither wiped up the spillage nor apologized for having caused it. She simply stood beside their table, one hand on her hip and the other hand holding her near-diminished cigarette.

"Y'all want anythang else?" she asked them, her voice a frigid country twang.

The *leader* of the two men spoke, "Would you mind putting a half teaspoon of cream in my coffee?"

The waitress hesitated slightly. "There's cream in that there jar," she told him, pointing at the cream that was sitting in the middle of the table. "You need a spoon or sumthin'?"

"No, I don't need a spoon, and I see the cream on the table. However, I'd prefer milk, if you don't mind?" he told her handing his cup of coffee to her.

"Milk?" she repeated.

He nodded his head.

She reluctantly grabbed the cup of coffee from him, spilling some of the hot brew onto her hand. Apparently, she was immune to the burning liquid because she didn't even flinch.

The two men laughed amongst themselves as they watched her mosey toward the kitchen. She returned quickly and set the coffee with a half-teaspoon of milk in front of the *leader*. She was noticeably cautious this time.

They kept silent as they sipped their coffee. Again, she stood beside their table waiting to see if either of them wanted anything else. Finally, convinced that they were content with their coffee, the waitress ambled her way back to the counter and resumed the camaraderie with the other waitress.

"From now on you are to refer to me as the *Good Samaritan,*" he calmly told the other man, still being careful to keep his voice low.

"*Good Samaritan*?" he mocked, surprised at the odd request.

"That is correct."

The other man chuckled. "May I ask why?"

The *Good Samaritan* took a sip of his coffee. "Let's just say that in essence, it is what my role has been over the years."

The other man shook his head. "As long as I'm gettin' my money, I don't care if you want me to call you *Buddha*!"

"*Good Samaritan* will be fine," he told him, nonchalantly.

"Then the *Good Samaritan* it is!"

"You also will be referred to by another name," he continued.

The other man's coffee cup aborted its ascension to his lips and landed quietly back onto the table. "Oh yeah?"

"Yes. From now on, I will refer to you as *Judas*."

"*Judas*?" he was even more surprised. "Hey, ain't that the dude that killed Jesus?"

"Something like that."

"How come the *brother* always got to be the bad dude?" he asked rhetorically.

"I don't see it that way. Besides, you will receive a decent pay for your efforts."

"Yeah, one-hundred-thousand-dollars worth of decency!"

Silence veiled their table momentarily.

"I only hope that I haven't made a bad decision in choosing to do business with you," the *Good Samaritan* uttered, a bit of apprehension clinging to his voice.

Judas tried to reassure him. "Naw, you ain't make no bad decision where I'm concerned."

He felt somewhat relieved. "Are you certain that everything will be in place so that it happens on *July twenty-fifth*? This is a special day for the airline."

"If that's the date you want it to happen, so be it. Don't worry 'bout a thing. This will be a piece of cake!"

"Fine. And as we agreed, one week before the mishap is scheduled to occur, you will receive fifty thousand dollars. You'll get the other half when the job is completed satisfactorily."

Judas grinned from ear-to-ear. "Hey, just out of curiosity, how many people suppose to be on this plane anyway?"

"That shouldn't concern you. It is probably best if you only concern yourself with making this thing happen," the *Good Samaritan* stated. "It will all be for the best in the long run."

"If you say so," *Judas* remarked.

The *Good Samaritan* glanced at his watch. "We'd better adjourn this little meeting - I do have an ad agency to get back to."

They both took one last sip of their coffee and then headed out the front door. As they entered into the warm air on this still early Monday morning hour, the *Good Samaritan* looked nervously up and down the street. Not that he was expecting to find anyone watching them. It was always better to be more careful than careless.

He shook hands with *Judas* and then waited inside his car watching as *Judas* drove away, heading south on the interstate. He then drove away in the opposite direction. And as he threaded his way through the rush-hour traffic starting to build, he pondered the agency's predicament. There was no way Prophet, Priest and King was going to come out on top of this review without him creating a major mishap.

He recalled the first one - a cruise ship explosion. It had stopped the review dead in its tracks. He then relived the second deadly mishap - a tainted pain reliever. And the most recent mishap had been the murder of a CorpAir executive.

There had never been any particular pattern or standard method for the mishaps. But he was about to begin one. It was time to repeat the first mishap - an explosion aboard one of its aircraft was exactly what was needed to divert CorpAir's attention away from this review.

All of the other incidents still remained unsolved mysteries. Nothing had ever gone awry. It had become the perfect panacea for dreaded account reviews. Everyone hated them. Unless of course, you were the agency trying to win the account from someone else.

Prophet, Priest and King essentially started with five accounts. They were all gained within the agency's first year of existence. Combined, the accounts represent annual billings of $100 million. Half of which were attributable to CorpAir. *Cygnificant Cruises* is the agency's second largest account at $20 million, followed closely by *Proxential Pharmaceutical* at $19 million; *SouthBanc* billed $8 million and *Quencher Beverages* billed $3 million. These five accounts were PPK's only accounts. They were dubbed the *PPK Five*.

The *Good Samaritan* knew that these accounts all needed to stay put. If the agency grew beyond their current $100 million in annual billings, then it would be due to the *PPK Five* increasing their budgets. The agency had no desire to chase after new business, and they sure as hell had no desire to lose any either.

He hoped that this would be the last time he'd have to engage in something like this. He tried not to think about the damage caused by the mishaps. In the long run jobs were saved, which ultimately affected lives. But he had no regrets. It was critical to him that the agency survive. Whatever the cost.

CHAPTER TWELVE

ADIVA ROBERTS SURPRISED JUST ABOUT everyone within the offices of Prophet, Priest and King by how quickly she was able to learn and successfully manage the agency's often frenetical switchboard. Rarely a day passed during her now three-weeks at the job when staffers weren't thanking her for a superb job she was doing in routing their calls correctly and handling the difficult ones professionally.

PPK was now one week away from making their initial presentation on the CorpAir review. It had been communicated to Adiva by Lorraine Brown to take messages for all the senior executives in the agency for the remainder of the week. Even if they were in their office and even if they were not on another line, no outside calls were to be put through.

Harvard, Duke and Princeton would be spending much of their time in the agency's executive conference room trying to put the finishing touch on their presentation. PPK's media VP – Seymour Boudreau, would accompany them; the head art director; a couple of copywriters; and both the account executive and account supervisor on the CorpAir account.

It was just after 2:00 on a Monday afternoon. Adiva was glad that the agency's switchboard was equipped with an *automated attendant*. The automated attendant, a recording that guided callers through a series of prompts, first answered the agency's incoming calls. Outside calls would come to her only if there was an overflow of calls or if someone pressed zero for the operator.

In between calls, Adiva found herself working on her

school's report. She didn't officially graduate from The Portfolio Institute until September, and the advertising report would have to be completed and graded prior to that time. She'd spent the weekend at the Georgia State University campus library looking through back issues of Advertising Age magazine to try and gather as much information about PPK as she could. There were more articles written about this agency than she had imagined. Especially interesting was an article written two years ago when PPK was named *Agency of the Year* by Advertising Age. It was a prestigious honor.

The feature was a cover story, complete with a full-color photograph of the PPK staffers assembled in front of the office building. Adiva found the article very intriguing. She was surprised to learn that since the agency's formation ten years ago they'd never lost a client. The agency had been asked to comment on the phenomenon within several of the articles that she'd read, but Harvard Prophet somehow detracted from the subject. It was as if he didn't want to talk about what appeared to be a great and rare accomplishment.

Adiva vowed to get more answers tomorrow morning when she was scheduled to meet with Harvard Prophet for a fifteen-minute interview before her day got started. Harvard initially rejected her request to have an interview with him, but later acquiesced with the condition that she take up no more than *fifteen* minutes of his time. Adiva had bargained for a one-hour interview, but after realizing that it wasn't going to happen, she agreed to the 7:45 a.m. *take-it* or *leave-it* offer from Harvard.

"Excuse me?" came the unfamiliar voice as Adiva read over her questions for tomorrow's interview. Standing before the receptionist workstation stood a very attractive, twenty-something woman with sandalwood-colored hair that was done into one long French braid that stretched beyond her slender shoulders, which happened to be exposed by the denim jumper she was wearing over a white blouse. Her chiseled face was slightly bronzed, revealing her recent affair at the tanning salon or soiree at the beach. And her demeanor failed to shield what Adiva detected as her propensity toward snobbery.

"May I help you?" Adiva asked, politely.

"My stars, did anyone ever tell you that you resemble *Jada Pinkett Smith*!" the young woman remarked in her noticeable southern diction.

Adiva blushed. The reference had been made many a times. "Yes, they have. And I'll take that as a compliment. Now, how may I help you?" she repeated.

"Of course, dahling! You see I'm expecting a call from London – from a Mr. Radford Albright. Will you be kind enough to page me if it comes in and I happen to be away from my desk?"

Adiva stared at her. "And you are?"

"Forgive me, dahling," she quickly apologized, extending her long bony, yet delicate arm across the receptionist's counter in an attempt to shake Adiva's hand. "We've never met. I'm Hannah."

Reluctantly, Adiva shook her hand. The reluctance wasn't out of a desire to be rude, but rather to protect her embarrassment of having sweaty palms. "Hi Hannah, I'm Adiva," she greeted.

"I know. Daddy told me that we had a new receptionist."

Daddy?

Hannah could see Adiva's bewilderment. "Harvard is my father," she began to explain. "I'm home from school for the summer. I'll be assisting my father with the agency during my break in classes."

Assisting in what? Adiva thought to herself, trying not to stare at the girl. But she could not see any resemblance to Harvard Prophet at all. In fact, she had assumed that Mr. Prophet would be a grandfather by now. Maybe she's adopted. Then again, she did know of couples who had decided to have their children later in life. Of course, in this instance, apparently it was much later for Harvard Prophet.

They continued to make small talk for a while longer. Adiva learned that twenty-two year-old Hannah Prophet was working on her MBA in marketing at a prestigious university in London.

"So, Hannah, how do you like living in London?" Adiva thought she'd ask, and hoping she wouldn't regret having done so. She did have a job to tend to.

Hannah's braided ponytail was lying across her shoulder. With her hand she tossed it behind her back. "Well, it is such a fascinating place to attend college, you know," she began. "But dahling, I don't believe that I've ever done so much work in one year than in my entire sweet life!"

Adiva bit her tongue. *Get behind me Satan.*

"I mean real hard work! The kind that puts pressure on the brain. Sometimes I felt like I was being squeezed between the mountains!"

Adiva was taken aback. *"Squeezed between the mountains?"*

"Of course. You know, a tough spot," Hannah attempted to explain.

Adiva couldn't keep from chuckling. "I think you mean *caught between a rock and a hard place,"* she corrected her.

Hannah's pretty face turned red. "Yes, of course." She remained silent as Adiva answered an incoming call.

"Sorry about that," Adiva told her, resuming their conversation. "So, is this Radford guy your boyfriend?"

Hannah appeared embarrassed. "Good heavens no!" she immediately protested. "Radford Albright is just a friend – a classmate of mine."

"Just asking," Adiva replied.

"He's a nice boy and all," Hannah continued. "I mean he does have such a remarkable misdemeanor."

Adiva shook her head in disbelief. "I think you mean *demeanor*."

"Pardon me?"

"*Misdemeanors* are usually associated with crimes. So, unless Mr. Albright has been charged with something less serious than a felony – in which case I don't know what would be so *remarkable* about it – I think you mean to say that the boy has a remarkable *demeanor,* not misdemeanor."

"I didn't need you to define the word for me," said Hannah tersely. "Anyway, I need for you to copy some files for me and then I need some supplies ordered."

Adiva listened quietly as Hannah rattled off the various tasks that she needed Adiva's assistance. She spoke with absolute authority. Adiva began to develop a dislike for her bossiness. She hoped that she wasn't planning on milking this *boss' daughter* thing for all it's worth. Finally, Adiva had to interrupt Hannah's plethora of demands. "Listen. These phones are starting to go crazy. And I'm supposed to check with Lorraine Brown before doing things outside of answering the phones, so you may want to discuss your requests with her first."

Hannah appeared offended. "Oh well. Maybe I can get some of them completed on my own. I just thought that you'd want to gain as much experience as you could. I mean you do have higher *allegations* than just answering the phones, don't you?"

Is this girl for real or what? Surely she means *aspirations.* But Adiva decided not to correct her this time. And to think the girl is studying abroad.

"Right now, my job is to answer the phones. And if you don't have any objections, Hannah, I need to get back to doing just that, okay?"

Hannah made an abrupt turn and walked hurriedly away.

Adiva was certain that she wasn't going to like this girl. If Hannah Prophet thought that just because she was the boss' daughter that she was going to order her around, then she had another thing coming. Hannah wasn't the first PPK staffer who'd tried to pawn some of their menial tasks off on her. Initially, she accepted the daunting work and completed it as best she could. But once Lorraine got wind of it, she quickly put an end to their clever antics.

The executive conference room at PPK was the most lavish of their three conference rooms. One of the four walls was all glass while the remaining three were constructed of cherry wood paneling. The enormous conference table was U-shaped, seating up to nineteen people. There were eight burgundy leather high-back chairs on each side of the 'U' and three additional chairs at the base of the 'U', which is where Harvard, Duke and Princeton each were seated.

There was a thirty-five-inch color television enclosed in the center of a wall unit. Surrounding the larger television were six smaller thirteen-inch sets - one to monitor commercials from each of the three major TV networks, one tuned to CNN, one tuned to the Golf Channel and the sixth one reserved for miscellaneous monitoring.

And since the executive conference room was directly across from the receptionist's area, the room was also sound proof so that those waiting outside in the reception area were not privy to anything being said inside.

Seymour Boudreau, PPK's media VP, had just finished his presentation on media plans for CorpAir. He was followed by Princeton King's creative presentation.

While everyone agreed that the new CorpAir ads, both print and television, looked great, Harvard was having a problem with the use of CorpAir's existing tagline on the new campaign.

"The *Up Where You Belong* tagline personifies the CorpAir brand," Princeton defended the theme.

"I'm quite aware of the significance of the tagline," Harvard grunted. "After all, I did write the damn line myself."

No one dared to argue with that fact.

Harvard continued, "My concern is that CorpAir has placed their account in review for a reason . . ."

"They want change," came a voice from someone on the media team.

"Exactly!" Harvard responded, pounding his fist on the table. "Which is why I find it difficult to see much *change* in continuing with their existing theme. I mean you can be damn sure that the boys in New York are planning to give CorpAir a *change*."

Harvard pushed his chair away from the conference table and stood. His bullish eyes began a slow but determined survey of his comrades seated around the room. "Ladies and gentlemen, we are the incumbent agency in this review. Whatever New York throws at CorpAir is going to come off as being fresh. This is why whatever we come up with has to be better than anything that we've ever created for CorpAir."

There were several heads nodding in agreement.

"We cannot rest on our laurels on this one," Harvard continued, his voice becoming more emphatic. "Prophet, Priest and King did not come this far to simply rest on our laurels! Make no mistake about it people, we will not lose this account! Not to New York, not to Chicago, not to anyone!"

The room erupted with applause.

As Harvard began a slow and methodical stroll around the conference room he spotted a young man who appeared to be bored stiff. He was a twenty-three year-old junior media executive. Although his boyish looks made him appear no more than sixteen.

As he persisted in playing with his tie - rolling it up until it stopped at his neck, and then finding a bit of amusement as he watched it fall freely down alongside the buttons of his shirt - he was oblivious to the fact that Harvard was standing directly behind his chair. By now, all eyes were drawn toward the young executive and his antics.

"Am I boring you, lad?" Harvard's boisterous words nearly caused the young man to wet on himself. He quickly composed himself, sitting up straight in his chair.

"Uh, no sir. Not at all."

Harvard placed his hands atop the young man's chair and gripped the leather with the force of his fingers. The lad dared to move. "What is your name?" he asked him. He hadn't met the recent recruit.

"Uh, Goldberg, sir. Allan Goldberg," he stammered.

"And how long have you been working for this agency, Mr. Goldberg?"

The young man cleared his throat. "Uh, just over one month, sir."

Because Harvard had a forceful grip on the chair, Allan Goldberg dared to move a muscle. He fixed his gaze straight ahead.

"Tell me, Mr. Goldberg . . . why is it that you do not seem interested in the fact that this ad agency – your *employer* for some four weeks – is faced with the distinct possibility of losing a $50 million account!"

Allan Goldberg felt faint. He could feel the harsh eyes of Harvard Prophet burning into the back of his skull. His armpits were drenched in perspiration. "Well, sir . . .from what I understand, this agency has never lost an account and . . . "

"And you don't believe that there's a first time for everything?" Harvard interrupted him intentionally.

"No, sir. I mean, well . . . Uh, I was sort of hoping that lady luck would be on our side again."

Seymour Boudreau, who was Goldberg's direct report, covered his face with his hand and bowed his head. His young protégé had just unknowingly slit his own throat.

Harvard's lips began to curl in disgust at the young man's response. His nostrils contracted reflexively. "Stand up, Mr. Goldberg!" Harvard demanded.

The young man complied without haste.

Harvard pulled Goldberg's chair from the table and shoved it down the aisle. It crashed into the wall.

He spun Goldberg around to face him. Trepidation littered the young man's flushing face. "Let me tell you something," Harvard began.

The room was deftly silent. Even the soft hum of the air conditioning system had paused momentarily, as if on cue.

"I've spent ten years of my life building this agency. We are *who* we are, and we are *where* we are because of many arduous efforts put forth within those ten years! And 'luck' has never had a damn thing to do with any of this agency's successes - do I make myself clear!"

Goldberg became speechless. He could feel the trap door opening in the pit of his stomach. He wished for the lever to be pulled to end his utter shame and embarrassment.

Harvard continued, "Now, I don't know where you worked before, Mr. Goldberg. But I can assure you that your mode of thinking is counter productive to the culture of this agency. And as such, I want you to take the next five minutes to gather up your personal belongings and then quietly remove yourself from these premises."

The lever indeed had been pulled.

As Allan Goldberg made his way hastily toward the door to exit the conference room, he heard Harvard's voice boom again. "You now have four minutes and thirty seconds, Mr. Goldberg!"

When the young man had disappeared from the room Harvard resumed his slow, steady stroll around the table. "Now, is there any one else feeling *lucky* today?" he asked with malicious delight.

Adiva wished that she were a fly on the wall as she observed Harvard Prophet strolling around the conference room. She could only speculate about the dejected-looking young man that minutes earlier had exited the meeting. She could not hear anything from her receptionist center, but she could tell from the looks on the many faces inside the conference room that the meeting was definitely intense.

At one point during his parade around the table, Harvard happened to catch Adiva staring. She quickly averted her gaze and immediately pretended to be answering a call. A short while later, it made no difference how much she stared because when she looked up from her desk Harvard had made a point to close all of the blinds on the glass windows; effectively shutting her out of their private gathering.

Adiva dialed Soupa Mann's work number at CorpAir. After only one ring she cancelled the call. She wasn't going to call him. He hadn't called her or come by her house since he failed to show up at church three weeks ago.

Well, she certainly had no intentions of calling him. She'd made her decision. If he had any hope of having a future with her, then he was going to have to start making some serious changes in his life –

spiritual changes. Adiva Roberts refused to creep any longer. Especially if it meant creeping with the enemy.

CHAPTER THIRTEEN

HER TUESDAY MORNING INTERVIEW with Harvard Prophet began promptly at 7:45. Adiva sat across from his massive mahogany desk in a plush side chair. Her time was limited so she decided to start with the key questions that she wanted answered. She cleared her throat. "First, I want to thank you for taking time out of your busy schedule for this interview," Adiva began. "Especially since the agency is in the midst of a major account review."

"You're quite welcome, Miss Roberts. I'm glad that you're able to appreciate my time constraints. And I'm flattered that you've chosen PPK as the subject matter for your school report." He paused. "Although I'm unable to devote much of my time to your efforts, I will do my best to provide you with as much valuable information as I can within the allotted time that we have. Is that fair enough?"

"Yes," Adiva answered. "It is." She shifted her posture in the chair. "Mr. Prophet, through my research on PPK, I have found it interesting that when you formed this agency ten years ago, during that first year you gained five clients, and all five of those clients are still on the roster today. And in fact, they remain the agency's only clients. Is this correct?"

"Most certainly," Harvard answered, beaming with pride. "The press dubbed them the *PPK Five*."

"Yes, I noticed that reference in one of the articles," she acknowledged. "Mr. Prophet, what's your secret? I mean, you've never lost a client in ten years nor have you sought to gain any additional clients aside from the initial five – why is that?"

Harvard stood from his big fat leather chair and strolled around his desk and seated himself in the side chair opposite Adiva. He crossed his legs. She couldn't help but notice the expensive loafers he was wearing. "Miss Roberts, the fact that we've never lost a client has absolutely nothing to do with any sort of secret or magic formula . . . "

Adiva quickly interjected, "I didn't mean to imply . . . "

Harvard held up his hand to stop her. "Allow me to continue, Miss Roberts. Please."

She relented.

"We are very good at what we do. Our five clients generate $100 million in annual billings. Now, I'm sure you'll agree that $100 million is nothing to sneeze at."

Adiva forced a smile.

Harvard continued to talk as he vacated the side chair opposite Adiva and returned to the high-back chair behind his desk. "As such, it has been my belief that in order to devote the proper time necessary to foster good client relations, five accounts are a suitable number relative to the size of this agency."

Adiva scribbled some notes on her notepad. "Mr. Prophet, is it safe to assume then, given PPK's proven success over the years, that you've actually turned away new clients?"

"Oh, absolutely!" he responded readily, as if the matter went without saying. "I suppose we've turned away . . . " He paused, trying to recall an exact figure. " . . . Oh I'm sure it's perhaps millions. However, I firmly believe that is the price that one has to pay if one is to maintain a track record that is unsurpassed."

Adiva managed an obligatory nod of her head.

"Make no mistake about it, Miss Roberts," he added. "We're very good at what we do."

"I don't doubt that, Mr. Prophet. But even the best agencies lose a client now and then. What makes PPK different from comparable agencies your size?"

"*Our* size," he corrected her. "You are now a part of this organization, Miss Roberts. Are you not?"

"Of course," she replied, unable to hide the embarrassment. "What makes *us* different from comparable agencies *our* size?" she rephrased the question.

"Miss Roberts, I have always believed that the advertising agency business has a lot to do with relationships. If you build good rapport with your clients or even potential clients, then you'll find that it goes a long way towards achieving not only your own goals, but those of your client as well."

"So, what you're saying is, the fact that PPK has never lost a client is due to its relationships with its clients?"

"To one extent, yes. But it goes much deeper than that." Harvard leaned back in his chair and propped his right leg on top of his left leg. "Allow me to be frank with you, Miss Roberts."

Adiva nodded her approval.

"I'm a very competitive individual. I don't take too kindly to losing at much of anything. I guess you might say that the primary reason why this agency has never lost a client is simply because I won't allow it to happen. I do not invest my time and resources to gain a particular advertiser only to turn around and lose that advertiser to someone else."

"But isn't that the way this business operates?" she asked. "I mean, clients move from one ad agency to the next all the time."

"True, but it hasn't always operated that way, Miss Roberts. Over the years other factors have entered the foray. Factors, which now practically preclude an agency from helping the client to achieve its objectives."

"What kind of factors?"

"Well, take these *search consultants*, for example. They were never heard of fifteen or twenty years ago. And if they were, their visibility was nil. But now, we've got these damn consultants all over the place! They're inducing clients to make agency changes simply for the sake of change. It's become absolutely ridiculous I tell you, absolutely ridiculous!"

Adiva observed the intensity in Harvard's voice. It was clear to her that this man held a deep passion for what he was doing. She continued to listen intently as Harvard addressed the *evils* that had changed the advertising agency business. He was on such a roll that he became oblivious to the time, which began to approach the half-hour mark. Adiva tried assiduously to write her notes within the fast pace manner in which he was speaking. It almost became too difficult for her to absorb all the information that he was spewing forth. But she wasn't about to call *time*.

Finally, she was able to get another question thrown in. "Mr. Prophet, CorpAir is our largest account, right?"

"Indeed, they are."

"From what I've gathered in my research, this particular account has grown from an initial $2 million in billings to its $50 million level today, correct?"

Harvard nodded in agreement.

"I've also discovered that CorpAir has undergone their share of executive management changes - especially at the marketing level - over the years. Now, aren't these the type of changes that usually bring about an agency review?"

He hesitated before answering. What was she driving at? Suddenly, he was beginning to resent this young woman's inquisition. She wanted to know more than what he felt she needed to know. "What exactly is your point, Miss Roberts?"

"Well, I'm just curious as to why CorpAir, considering their previous changes in management personnel during PPK's tenure, never sought an agency review at one time or another before now?"

"I never said that a review wasn't ever sought. As a matter of fact, three of our largest clients have put their accounts up for review during their tenure with us."

Interesting, Adiva thought to herself. "So then, apparently PPK was successful in defending those accounts because they're still on the roster?"

Harvard loosened his tie and then the button on his shirt collar. "Let's just say that the reviews never took place."

"I don't understand what you mean," she stated, leaning forward in her chair.

"None of the account reviews took place because . . . " Before Harvard could finish his sentence, his telephone buzzed. He motioned with his hand for Adiva to wait a moment while he answered the call. "I'm terribly sorry, Miss Roberts. But I'm afraid we're going to have to call it quits. I must take this phone call," he explained, after identifying the caller.

"Sure, I understand," she acknowledged, gathering up her things. She really wished that he'd have finished the last sentence. She glanced at her watch and noticed that it was 8:17. Lorraine was probably covering for her up front. She hurried down the corridor toward the receptionist area.

There was a certain mystique surrounding this agency's phenomenal success. Her interest had been magnified even more after meeting with Harvard Prophet. She realized that she would simply have to dig deeper to try and unravel the tangled questions that were beginning to consume her.

Princeton King was having a difficult time concentrating on the CorpAir review. His body had begun to feel the pressures of trying to save the agency's largest client. For the past three weeks he'd put away a six-pack of Bud Light each day during a one-hour period. And during lunch he chose to recluse himself within his office with the door locked. For the most part he went through his usual routine – drink the beer; smash the cans, empty the waste basket; place the flattened beer cans in a large manila envelope and then put the envelope at the bottom of the waste basket before refilling it with the trash.

This afternoon, however, he skipped *smashing-the-cans* part. Princeton felt that he didn't even have the strength to stomp on an ant. So, the empty beer cans were simply thrown into his wastebasket and covered up with the other trash.

He told himself that these episodes had to come to an end soon. He realized that if Muriel ever found out that he was drinking again, his marriage would essentially be over. The two of them were already on shaky ground and she was looking for any excuse to take the kids and make a mad rush back to Chicago. She really never wanted to come to Atlanta.

Princeton dozed in and out of sleep as he sat practically slumped over his desk. A knock at the door startled him. Quickly, and half-dazed, he tried to regain his composure. Papers were shuffled about. He ran his fingers through his hair. "Who is it?" he called out, being careful not to slur his speech.

"It's Adiva," came the soft answer.

"Um, okay. Wait a moment. I'm finishing up a phone call," he lied, unashamedly.

"I can come back another time," he heard her say, as he attempted to make himself presentable.

"I'll be right there." Princeton unlocked the office door and invited her in. He wondered if the office smelled of beer and if she noticed the smell.

It did and she had.

However, Adiva thought nothing of it. The man was a partner in the agency. He could do whatever he felt like doing.

"I'm sorry to interrupt you," she told him.

"Think nothing of it," Princeton assured her, his speech slurring slightly. "What's on your mind?"

"Well, you told me during my interview that you would be willing to assist me," she reminded him.

"Assist you?"

"Yes. My school paper – I'm doing a report on PPK," she tried to jog his memory.

"Oh, of course! The report you have to complete for The Portfolio Institute. Forgive me but I completely forgot."

Adiva smiled at him.

"I'll be glad to help out any way I can. What do you need to know?"

Adiva sat down in the same chair in which she sat in three weeks ago to interview with him. She discussed with Princeton her earlier interview with Harvard. She explained to him that because of time constraints Harvard wasn't able to complete the interview and that she was hoping maybe he could fill in some of the gaps.

Princeton was more than willing to be of assistance. He needed a respite from the day's toils.

"Before my interview this morning with Mr. Prophet was cut short, we were discussing PPK's account reviews with the three largest clients and how the agency was able to stay agency-of-record. Can you elaborate on this?"

Princeton scratched the top of his red head. "Well, we've never had a major issue with reviews. I mean, we only have five accounts," he chuckled to himself. "It is true that three of our largest clients have placed their accounts up for review at one time or another. And, well, fortunately for us, the reviews never took place."

Adiva looked puzzled. "What do you mean *never took place?*"

Princeton appeared apprehensive about discussing the subject. He plopped his feet onto his desk. "Well, to make a long story short, each of the three clients - Cygnificant Cruises, Proxential Pharmaceutical and CorpAir, had their account up for review all at different times. And before the review process could be completed, something happened that caused the client to either delay or scuttle the review altogether."

Adiva's interest grew. "What happened?"

"Well, in the case of Cygnificant Cruises, there was a major explosion aboard one of its ships, many passengers died. It was a nightmare for the client as well as for us. The review ended up taking a back seat. The agency immediately went into damage control and eventually restored the client's standing among its customers."

Adiva shook her head. "That's unbelievable."

"And ironically, similar incidents occurred with the other two clients. That is to say, Proxential Pharmaceutical was faced with a major consumer scare when some of their products were found to be laced with cyanide; and of course, the first time CorpAir placed its account up for review five years ago, just before final presentations were due, their marketing chief was murdered."

"Do you believe that these incidents were all coincidences?" Adiva asked.

"Well, that's not for me to say. Duke, Harvard and I have discussed it amongst ourselves before, but basically, they were all separate and unique incidents. I guess we've been very fortunate."

Adiva glanced at her notes. "The agency is one week away from making its initial presentation, and the final presentations aren't due until August - what are the chances of this review being cancelled?"

"It's been five years since we've even faced a review. Personally, I'm convinced that those earlier incidents were just that - incidents. CorpAir is ready to change agencies. The time is ripe for it. Somehow I don't think that we're going to be as fortunate."

This was all getting more and more incredible, Adiva thought. She noticed that her break was almost over so she quickly switched gears. "Princeton, if you don't mind me asking, I know that there are three agency partners - how are the percentages split?"

He hesitated. "Well, I don't suppose there's any big secret about it. Harvard, of course, is the majority partner with a seventy-percent stake, and Duke and I maintain a fifteen-percent stake each."

"So, Mr. Prophet pretty much runs the show, huh?"

"That he does! And, he'd like nothing more than to get his hands on the remaining thirty-percent stake as well," Princeton remarked, unable to restrain his thoughts.

"What are the chances of that happening?"

"Zilch if I can help it. But I think Duke's about ready to cash in." Princeton shared with Adiva his recent discussion with Duke Priest about giving up his partnership status within the agency. He told her that he was quite sure that Duke would give him first option to purchase his fifteen-percent stake instead of selling back to the old man. He then realized that he might have divulged more information than he should have. It was obvious that the beers were doing the talking for him.

Adiva realized that her afternoon break had extended way beyond her allotted time. She politely thanked Princeton for his cooperation before heading back to the receptionist area. He complimented her on her probing skills.

After she'd departed from his office, Princeton tried to devote his attention back to the CorpAir review. He questioned himself as to why he was exerting so much energy into trying to save the account. He knew in his heart that their days as agency-of-record for CorpAir were numbered. And just like so many agencies facing reviews today, it was only a matter of time before their number was going to be called.

CHAPTER FOURTEEN

MOST OF THE PPK STAFFERS HAD departed for the day. Harvard Prophet was sitting on the plush leather sofa in his office reading the day's *Wall Street Journal* while one of Aretha Franklin's classic tunes played soothingly in the background. He was apprehensive about the first round of presentations that were scheduled for next Monday. Harvard accepted the fact that the first round of presentations for the CorpAir review would go on as scheduled. Nothing was going to stop the presentations from occurring. However, he realized that it had to end there.

He was quite confident that PPK would survive the initial round. CorpAir would want them around until the very end. At least then it could appear that the PR-conscious airline had tried hard to keep their account with them. But Harvard was not naïve. And he was no fool. If the CorpAir review carried through to the final round, PPK was as good as dead. There was no plausible way that they would remain agency-of-record. In fact, Harvard believed that CorpAir, for the most part, already knew whom they wanted as their new ad agency. These reviews were nothing more than politics. Which is why he was never more certain that something had to occur to derail this review all together. Whatever was necessary to stop it, it had to be done.

He gently folded the MONEY & INVESTING section of the *Journal* and set it aside. He checked the time on his watch. It was *7:30* on a Tuesday evening. He walked, in his usual cool and hip fashion, over to his office door and locked it. He went and stood in front of the wall that was adjacent to his sitting area and carefully removed a *Picasso* that hung sturdily from the wall. Behind the expensive painting was a rectangular doorbell size button affixed to the wall. He put forth his index finger and depressed the button. Immediately the wall slid open and Harvard stepped inside the small-darkened room. He flipped the light switch, illuminating the room.

TV monitors lined the wall. Voice-recording machines turned continuously. No one other than himself knew about this room. He called it his *Intelligence Center.* Hidden cameras and microphones were placed within the offices of each of his senior staff members, including the offices of Duke Priest and Princeton King. At the end of each day, when he was certain that everyone else had left the premises, he would review the tapes. What they did and or said behind the closed doors of their offices was not unbeknownst to him. He knew what they thought about their jobs. He was privy to their problems at home. He was keenly aware of their feelings on the

CorpAir review. And, more importantly, Harvard knew what they thought about him.

He pulled the tape of Princeton King's affairs for the day. He shook his head in disgust as he watched Princeton drown himself in beers, drinking the afternoon away. *What an absolute idiot,* Harvard thought to himself. Princeton King didn't deserve to own fifteen-percent of his agency or any other agency for that matter. *It was perhaps time to put a little pressure on Mr. King,* he grinned.

He quickly scanned the videotapes from the offices of Duke Priest, Seymour Boudreau, a couple of creative heads, his human resources director and his vice president of finance. And as always, if the tapes contained scenes or if information was uttered that he deemed pertinent, the tapes were labeled and saved. Otherwise he simply recorded over them again.

Prior to his completion of reviewing the day's tapes, Harvard dubbed a copy of the scene that showed Princeton King drinking himself silly. He then placed a blank label on the tape and wrote across the labeling strip - *For Your Eyes Only.* The VHS videotape was then placed into his attaché case.

As he prepared to exit the *Intelligence Center,* he set the timers on the machines to begin recording again tomorrow morning. The lights were turned off and the wall closed up again. The Picasso was once again hung neatly in place on the wall.

Harvard peeked at his watch. He was scheduled to pick up Hannah within an hour for dinner. He quickly shoved some file folders into his attaché case and slammed it shut. He popped the Aretha Franklin disk from the CD player was quickly out the door.

◈◈◈◈◈◈◈

After returning home from their Wednesday night Bible class, Adiva and Granny Rae were relaxing in their living room sharing a large bowl of popcorn. The TV was on but neither or them were giving it any attention. Granny Rae was flipping the pages of the latest *National Enquirer,* while Adiva found herself trying to concentrate on her research report for The Portfolio Institute.

Part of the problem for Adiva's lack of concentration on her research report was due to the fact that she was allowing her anger towards Soupa Mann to intensify. He still had not contacted her. Although she knew that nothing bad had happened to him because for the past two Mondays she'd been calling his job and asking to speak to him. But before he could answer the phone, she'd already hung up. At least she knew a car or something hadn't hit him.

Adiva was angry with herself for feeling the way she did. *He* was the one who didn't show up for church three weeks ago. Why was she feeling guilty? Why was she so anxious to call him? He should have called her long before now and begged her forgiveness. She wondered how he could be so trifling.

"You need to just forget him, Diva," Granny Rae piped in, sensing her granddaughter's mood. "He ain't no good," she added, not even glancing up from her tabloid.

"What are you talking about Granny Rae?" Adiva responded, even though she was fully aware of what her grandmother was speaking of.

"Chile you knows what grandma is talkin' 'bout. Let that soup fella be – find yo self a *good* man, Diva."

"Granny Rae, I'm not even thinking about Soupa Mann," she lied.

"I knows you is. And you knows it too. But honey, ain't no man worth sacrificing yo happiness."

Adiva remained silent.

Granny Rae put the tabloid aside. "I've been down them roads before, Diva," she continued. "I knows I was brought up during a diff'rent time and all, but I done traveled them roads just the same."

"Things are a lot different today, Granny Rae," Adiva attempted to defend herself and Soupa Mann.

"Sure they are, Chile. But ain't nothin' diff'rent 'bout them roads. Now, the names of the streets may have changed, but that's all. 'Cause I tell you, Diva, them roads ain't no diff'rent today than theys was in my day."

Maybe her grandmother was right. The surroundings may have changed, but when you get right down to it, the world isn't any different today than it was fifty years ago - in terms of the problems you have to deal with. Besides, things always happened for a reason. *That,* she believed wholeheartedly.

After all, what kind of future could she possibly expect to have with Soupa Mann if he didn't respect her enough to call her and tell her that he wouldn't be coming to church? And how could they expect to live in harmony with one another when their beliefs and moral values were so diametrically opposed? His continual lack of interest in spiritual matters should have been the handwriting on the wall for her. But Adiva didn't want to give up on him so easily. Granted, she realized that she was in love with the man, but she also realized that he had a soul. A soul that was in need of salvation. Maybe God put him in her life for that very purpose. Who was she to try and go against God's will?

Guilt settled over her as she recalled the last of the three times that she'd given herself to Soupa Mann. She knew it was scripturally wrong to engage in intimacy outside of the marriage relationship. But during those intimate moments it became all too clear to her that the flesh could manifest enormous power over the spirit. And it was that power in which she regrettably surrendered to.

Maybe that's why Soupa Mann no longer respected her. Granny Rae had always taught her to be careful about giving herself away for free. And of course, she knew the saying all to well – *why buy the cow if you can get the milk for free?*

"Are you hearing me, Chile?" Granny Rae's voice suspended her silence.

"Yes, Granny Rae. I hear what you're saying," Adiva answered. "But I don't just care about him as a man, I care about his soul too," she protested.

"Diva, that fella don't care nothin' 'bout his own soul. You can't be saved for him . . . nobody can. He gots to want to save his self."

Adiva resented the fact that her grandmother was speaking of Soupa Mann as if he was a heathen of some kind. He wasn't that bad of a guy. Yes, he smoked cigarettes but he didn't do drugs and he doesn't get crazy drunk. There were no doubt people who called themselves *Christians* who probably did a lot worse.

Granny Rae could see the anguish and pain within her granddaughter. "Diva, I just wants whats best for you. Yo momma and daddy would've wanted nothin' less for you themselves," she quietly stated. "Now, I knows it won't be long before the Good Lord calls me home and . . . "

"Don't talk like that Granny Rae," Adiva interrupted.

"Naw Chile, you knows it's the honest truth. And I'm ready when calls for me. And when I goes, Diva, I don't want to leave you knowin' that you all worried 'bout some man."

Adiva realized that it would be pointless to continue this conversation with her grandmother. Especially since Granny Rae was probably right about everything she had said.

The sound of the doorbell's chime resonated throughout the house. "I'll get it," Adiva said, rising from the sofa and making a quick note of the *9:27 p.m.* time on her watch as she wondered whom it could be at the door.

As she unlocked the two dead bolts and then opened the front door, she was pleasantly surprised to see Soupa Mann standing before her. He was wearing a beige collarless silk shirt and he had both of his hands shoved into the front pockets of his black trousers. She wanted to throw her arms around him and kiss his face and tell him how much she missed him. Instead, she kept her emotions under restraint.

"Well, do I at least get a *hello*?" Soupa Mann teased, flashing his made-for-TV Bel Air smile.

Adiva thought about saying something nasty and sarcastic to him, but she couldn't find the exact words. "Hi Soupa Mann," she spoke, a dry swallow escaping her. She was relieved that he couldn't see her heart swelling with enthusiasm at his presence. "What are you doing here?" she asked, not necessarily caring for an answer to the question because the fact-of-the-matter was – he *was* here.

"I came to see you," he answered with an incriminating look in his eyes.

"Why the long wait?"

Soupa Mann's face suddenly displayed a pitiful look of appeal. " 'Cause I been doing some thinking," he responded.

"About what?"

"Mainly us. But also about my own life. You know, the direction I'm headed . . . my future . . . *our* future. Changes I need to make"

Adiva gave him a slow, appraising glance. She attempted to scrutinize every inch of his handsome face in search of clues that he was or wasn't being sincere. He knew all too well just the right words to say to try and get himself out of trouble. And she didn't want to fall into his subtle trappings. But her strong emotional bond with him eventually rendered her judgment acutely partial. She decided to hear what he had to say.

Adiva invited him inside the house.

When Granny Rae saw whom it was that had intruded on her conversation with her granddaughter, she suppressed the indignation welling up inside her.

Soupa Mann uttered a nervous, yet polite hello to Granny Rae. And even he could detect the spasm of irritation crossing Granny Rae's face as she rolled her eyes at him. She chose to say nothing to him. Instead, Granny Rae grabbed hold of her walker and doddered from the den into her bedroom.

"She hates my guts," Soupa Mann remarked, after he was certain that Granny Rae was out of earshot.

The two of them sat down on the sofa. "It's not so much that she hates *you,*" Adiva tried to soften the reaction. "its just hat she cares a lot about *me.*"

Soupa Mann quickly took offense. "And I don't care about you?"

"You tell me?" Adiva shot back. "You're the one who promised to attend church with me and then didn't even bother to show up!"

Soupa Mann sunk deeper into his guilt and shame. "I wanted to be there, but . . . "

"But what, Soupa Mann?" Adiva wasn't trying to hear his lame excuses. Yes, she was glad to see him, but she was also still very angry over being stood up and disrespected.

"Something . . . "

She interrupted his reply. "Did you stay out all night partying – is that it?"

He grew defensive. "Hey, when you left The Bronze Peach I was right behind you!"

"Yeah, right. Did you oversleep then?"

He let out an exasperated sigh. "No, I didn't oversleep. Something came up all right. It was a business situation that I had to take care of."

"On a Sunday morning?" she questioned him, her eyes narrowing speculatively.

"Yeah, that's right. On a Sunday morning."

"I'm not even trying to hear that, Soupa Mann. You had no intentions of coming to church with me, so don't insult my intelligence with your lies!"

"I ain't lying," he said, unconvincingly.

Adiva turned up her nose and sniffed the air. "Have you been smoking? Because you smell like smoke," she accused him.

"I told you I was quitting, didn't I?"

"You've told me a lot of things, Soupa Mann."

"Why you jumping all over me, Adiva?"

"I'm not jumping on you. If you'll remember, we talked about your smoking habit many times – it's dangerous to your health! Or don't you even care?"

"Well, the pain I been feeling lately ain't coming from smoking cigarettes!"

"What do you mean by that?"

He fanned the air with his hand. "Nothing. Just forget I even said anything."

Except for the dialogue emanating from the television, silence filled the widening gap between them.

As much as Adiva missed Soupa Mann, she'd grown tired of his empty promises and never-ending excuses. She understood that, generally, people didn't change overnight – if they changed at all. Soupa Mann was a grown man. If this was the type of person he chose to be, then who was she to try and change him – or even think that she was capable of doing so?

Maybe they were just two different types of yokes. Unequal to one another. And as Brother Blake's sermon had so eloquently pointed out, Christians were not to be unequally yoked.

"You'd better be leaving," Adiva told Soupa Mann, collapsing the silence. "I've got to get up early for work in the morning."

"Yeah, okay," he responded, getting up from the sofa. "We can talk some more later."

Adiva didn't acknowledge his last statement. What was left for them to discuss? She led him to the front door and opened it. He stood in front of it, head bowed in apparent defeat with his hands thrust in his front pockets. He made a weak attempt to give her a kiss on the cheek, but she quickly backed away, giving him a dismissive gesture.

As Soupa Mann walked slowly to his Jeep, he heard the door close and lock behind him. When he reached the car he dug his hand into his hip pocket and removed the packet of *Benson & Hedges.* He tapped the pack on his other hand to dispense one of the cigarettes. He stuck the white stick between his lips and lighted it. He slowly blew the smoke into the cool nighttime air and watched as the smoke evaporated into nothingness.

Then he removed the cigarette, with its tip a glowing red, from his mouth and just stared at it. There had to be more to life, he thought to himself. More to life than this rolled up tobacco that you puffed on day in and day out, trying to derive whatever pleasure from it that you could.

He allowed the cigarette to fall from his fingers to the ground. As it landed against the concrete driveway it still burned. He watched it smolder a few seconds before placing his size nine sandal on top of it and grinding it to smithereens.

CHAPTER FIFTEEN

ONE MONTH HAD PASSED SINCE CORPAIR had publicly announced a review of their $50 million advertising account that was currently being handled by Prophet, Priest and King. Harvard Prophet realized that time didn't appear to be on his side. While he was somewhat relieved that PPK had made it past the first round of presentations, he actually expected it. And now, with that onerous phase behind him, and the Fourth of July holiday over, it became incipient to him that they were right in the thick of things.

CorpAir had reduced the number of agencies in contention for their account down to three from eight. PPK was up against two industry behemoths - New York's *Young & Lucas* and *Graystone Advertising*. Both agencies raked in annual billings somewhere within the billion-dollar range. The scales certainly were not tilted in his favor. He wondered how CorpAir's CEO, Douglas Sheldon, could seriously think that PPK would be able to compete in this arena. There was absolutely no way that CorpAir could possibly be viewing PPK as a viable contender. They were obviously stringing them along merely for show. And had it not been for his personal relationship with

Douglas Sheldon, PPK might not have even been invited to participate in the review.

In less than sixty days he was expected to give the presentation of his life in an attempt to save the agency's future.

Why hadn't he seen this review coming? The year thus far had seen an enormous amount of activity within the ad industry. More than thirty major accounts worth over $2 billion had changed hands over the past six months alone. Few, if any, of the major shops escaped their clients' wrath.

Harvard sat quietly in his office and tried to make sense of it all. He swallowed hard as he tallied up the time and energy he'd spent building and cementing what he thought was a solid relationship with Douglas Sheldon. After all, that was how it was suppose to work.

The country club membership, the chairmanship of the *Atlanta Association of Advertising Agencies,* and the vice-presidency of the *Atlanta Commerce Association,* had all secured for Harvard Prophet a place within the *good ol' boy* network. But something happened to change the landscape. He recalled Douglas' words that CorpAir wanted to "shake things up a bit." Was this some sort of *game* that advertisers enjoyed playing? CorpAir was his *baby* – his first-born. It was his to raise and to nurture. How could he possibly allow an *outsider* to come in and simply take away a member of his *family*?

Harvard's thoughts turned to his twenty-two year-old daughter, Hannah. The time and effort that he'd poured out raising her was now exemplified by his daughter's academic excellence, her indisputable mannerisms and her utmost respect for him. Through his guidance and direction Hannah Prophet had turned out to be very mature woman. His dream had always been to hand the agency's reins over to his daughter one day. But now, that dream was about to be turned into a nightmare.

He opened the center drawer of his desk. He carefully lifted the wooden pencil tray that was positioned snugly in place and removed a small silver key from underneath. The key fit the bottom right-side drawer of his desk. Harvard inserted the key and pulled the drawer forward to open it. He removed a red letter-size file folder. Across the top of the folder were the printed words *MISHAPS*. He put on his *Ben Franklin* reading glasses and began perusing the file.

The contents consisted of copies of newspaper articles. There were three of them. All of them had run as front-page stories in the Atlanta Post-Gazette. He looked at the headline of the most recent article. It was dated February 17, 1995 - LOCAL MARKETING EXECUTIVE SLAIN WHILE JOGGING NEAR HIS HOME LAST NIGHT. The man had been CorpAir's chief marketing officer who was heading up the review of CorpAir's then $35 million account. The incident threw the entire review into limbo. Harvard had seized the opportunity to convince Douglas Sheldon to postpone the impending review. He did. And subsequently it was never rescheduled. Until last month.

Harvard retrieved the second article from the file. It was dated seven years ago - *November 20, 1993.* Its third current largest client at that time as well as now, was Proxential Pharmaceutical. The client had decided to place its account up for review citing "creative differences" with PPK. Proxential had only been with the agency for three months. Harvard realized that it would have been humiliating to lose an account that soon after having been awarded it.

This one came down to the wire. It was a close call. Less than thirty days before final presentations were to be given - and PPK had not made the final cut - the mishap occurred and saved the account. He stared at the headline - PROXENTIAL PAIN PILLS KILL THREE IN BOSTON AND TWO IN SEATTLE. The client had a major catastrophe on its hands. Their over-the-counter pain reliever had been laced with cyanide poisoning. The company's stock began to sink faster than the *Titanic.* Stores from across the country began a frantic race to remove the product from its shelves. It was a public relations and advertising nightmare. And so in an effort to try and put out the many fires starting to rage, PPK was quickly restored as agency-of-record. The account now bills $19 million and it has never been up for review since.

Harvard removed the last article. It was dated nine years ago - July 10, 1991. PPK had just recently celebrated their one-year anniversary. The headline was in big black bold type – MAJOR EXPLOSION ABOARD CYGNIFICANT CRUISE SHIP - OVER ONE HUNDRED PASSENGERS KILLED. Cygnificant Cruises is PPK's second largest account. At the time of this incident, the account was up for review. Two days before the first round of presentations were scheduled to take place, the explosion aboard one of its ships occurred. Again, Harvard was successful at getting the client to scrap the review. Cygnificant Cruises needed to regain public trust. PPK had been successful with the account up to that point so it was only fitting that they be allowed to salvage their client's tarnished image.

Harvard knew he was fortunate. His agency was fortunate. Three of his five accounts had been brought back from the brink. The other two accounts, to date, have never been up for review.

Unbelievable. Yet it was proven. He had the proof in his hands. Stop a review dead in its tracks with the onset of major chaos or some kind of mishap.

Harvard thought about the young Goldberg's words – *lady luck*. Not in his agency. That is why he was the leader of PPK. In the face of defeat stare it down! Bring it into subjection! His accounts were never meant to leave his agency. And rightly so. He grew them and he was planning to continue growing them. It was his responsibility – his duty – to keep the *PPK Five* alive!

He replaced the articles into the red folder and returned it to the drawer. He locked the drawer and concealed the little key beneath the pencil tray inside his center desk drawer.

It was good for him to have revisited those articles. Those encouraging stories. He was glad that he had saved them over the years. They gave him hope.

CorpAir would not be going anywhere. He deeply regretted the fact that they'd chosen to tempt fate by placing their account up for review. He was certain that CorpAir's addition of Christine Armstrong as VP of Marketing was the driving force behind this review. It had become an all too frequent occurrence within the industry. Harvard knew and understood that one of the primary reasons an agency review occurred was due to a change in management on the client side. It never failed. Whether it was a new CEO or a change in marketing leadership, it more than likely meant that an agency review loomed on the horizon.

He thought about the two mega shops in New York - Y&L and Graystone. They were probably salivating at the chance to snare the coveted CorpAir brand. Why couldn't they chase bigger fish - the *AT&Ts*, the *GMs* or the *Revlons*? He wished that they both would just go away - leave his $50 million account alone!

Harvard realized, however, that all the blame for this review didn't rest with greedy and aggressive ad agencies. The *client* shared in this upheaval. Just because the big New York shops came courting

CorpAir didn't mean that CorpAir had to agree to dance with them. They could have refused. They could have told the big boys that they weren't interested. Explain to them that they'd been happily married for years. But they chose not to. CorpAir listened to the big boys' overtures. Accepted their invitations to dinner. Gave credence to their *'what if'* scenarios. CorpAir could have simply stood their ground, but instead they folded wittingly like a deck of cards in the hands of a Las Vegas casino dealer.

Duke Priest was on the phone with a senior executive at SouthBanc, an $8 million account on PPK's roster - number four of the *PPK Five*. The client was concerned about the negative impact that the potential loss of CorpAir's $50 million account would have on the advertising agency, and ultimately on his own account with the agency.

Duke could feel the apprehension in the client's quivering voice. When the forty-five minute conversation finally concluded, it was perspicuous to him that if CorpAir walked away from PPK, SouthBanc's $8 million account was planning to follow them out the door as well.

He sat motionless at his desk. He was debating whether or not to inform Harvard of his conversation with SouthBanc. Duke realized that Harvard had enough pressure on him as it was.

Adding another block of bad news to an already shaky foundation was the last thing that he wanted to do. He rationalized that even if Harvard was told about the threat from SouthBanc there would be very little he could do about it at the moment. The likelihood of losing a $50 million account certainly took precedent over the likelihood of losing $8 million.

Duke Priest was ninety-nine percent certain that PPK was going to lose CorpAir during the final round of presentations. Their success with this one account over the years had been the catalyst of their overall success. He'd always felt uneasy about Harvard's flagrant desire to ride on the wings of CorpAir's enormous success. The agency should have never allowed itself to become so dependent upon a single client. Now, the very future of the agency was resting in the hands of its largest account.

He decided that he would not breathe a word of his conversation with SouthBanc to Harvard. And while he had his doubts, he realized that PPK could not lose CorpAir as a client.

They hadn't faced a review of any kind in five years. Why now? The business was hard enough without the prospect of losing $50 million of your annual billings.

He'd had enough of agency reviews, client threats, and an eccentric and egotistical old man. His wife had divorced him largely due to his inability to separate business from personal matters. But he'd always felt obligated. He owed it to the agency to invest all of his energy into making it a success. Yet, no other effort had ever caused him so much stress and agony. The decision to sacrifice his personal life for his career had been a steep price to pay.

And yet, it appeared that his work was still not quite finished.

CHAPTER SIXTEEN

ON TUESDAY JULY 7th, IT WAS ALMOST 10:15 when Lorraine Brown finally arrived to relieve Adiva from the switchboard so that she could take her 10:00 morning break. When she arrived she apologized profusely to Adiva for being late. She explained that she had been in a meeting with Harvard Prophet. And to compensate for her tardiness she allowed Adiva to add an extra ten minutes to her fifteen-minute break.

Adiva gladly accepted the offer. She'd already planned to use PPK's library to try and gather more information on the agency and its clients for her school report. She had an interesting and frightening theory swirling around in her head. One that she'd only felt comfortable sharing with Princeton King.

As she walked down the narrow corridor toward PPK's library, she could see Hannah Prophet approaching. *Oh, lord. The boss' daughter.* Silently, she cursed Lorraine, because if Lorraine had not been late in relieving her from the switchboard she would already be in the library by now instead of having to confront her nemesis. As the two women neared one another, Adiva hoped that Hannah would simply speak and keep on walking.

No such luck.

Hannah was the first to speak as the two women stood face-to-face. "Good morning, Reba."

"It's *Adiva,*" she was quick to correct her.

"Sorry," Hannah mumbled, her embarrassment palpable.

"No problem," she lied. "Good morning to you."

They stood in awkward silence briefly. "Um, Adiva, dahling . . . " Hannah spoke first again. " . . . about the other day . . . "

"What about it?"

"Well, we kind of got off to a bad start . . . "

"And?" Adiva interrupted her.

"Well, I thought that maybe we could meet for lunch this afternoon. You know, dahling, sort of start over."

Adiva was skeptical. After all, she could only wonder what ulterior motive Hannah had for wanting to get on her good side. If anyone should be trying to butter-up to someone, it certainly shouldn't be the boss' daughter. "You want to have lunch with me?"

"That is, if you don't already have other plans."

Adiva thought for a moment. "I only get one hour for lunch, and I was hoping to work on my school report during my lunch at the agency's library."

Hannah appeared disappointed. Then her face brightened. "Well, you could always use our library!" she offered, cheerfully.

"Excuse me?"

"I mean, the library at our house. It's filled with memorabilia on this agency. And after lunch, I could lend you a hand in finding what you're looking for. You know what they say – one head doesn't get much better than two!"

Adiva allowed a chuckle to escape. "That's *two heads are better than one*!"

"I was close."

"Let me make sure I understand – you are inviting *me* to have lunch with *you* at your house – the *Prophet Palace*?"

"Oh, don't be silly! It's not really a palace," Hannah said modestly.

"To someone like me, it is!" Adiva assured her. "I have seen pictures of that estate."

Neither of them could contain their laughter. "Besides, *Miss Thing*, how do you propose that I do all of this within one hour? You may be the boss' daughter, but I actually *work* here!"

"Well, dahling, don't be upset with me, but I've already spoken to Lorraine and she's agreed to give you an extra hour for lunch."

Unbelievable, Adiva thought. "You've already spoken to my boss about letting me take a two-hour lunch break?"

"Yes. And she said it was okay. I hope that I wasn't being assumptuous."

Adiva shook her head. "Girl, you mean *presumptuous*."

"Yes, that."

Adiva couldn't believe what she was hearing. Hannah was chatting with her as if they'd been girlfriends for years. Not so long ago Hannah was treating her like she was some second class citizen. Now all of a sudden she wanted to have her in her home for lunch. Adiva wondered what exactly brought about this one hundred and eighty-degree change in attitude? She would have thought that Hannah would be trying to get together with her own friends after just getting back into the country.

Although, Adiva was curious about the possibility of seeing the Prophet Palace up close. She remembered that the estate was recently featured in an issue of *Atlanta Homes and Lifestyles* magazine.

"Okay, Hannah. I'll join you for lunch."

"Great!" Hannah nearly shouted. "I'll call up Sebastian and tell him to have lunch prepared for us around noon."

"And who is Sebastian?"

But before Hannah could answer, Adiva replied, "Let me guess – he's the chef?"

Hannah giggled. "Yes. He's daddy's butler and cook."

"Oh, well pardon me," Adiva teased.

By the time the two of them had finished conversing, Adiva's morning break was over. She was somewhat disappointed that she didn't even make it to the library. But she was now eagerly anxious for lunchtime to roll around. This was bound to be the most intriguing luncheon that she'd ever been invited to attend.

Princeton King looked over the three newspaper articles that Adiva had copied from the Georgia State University library over the weekend. Adiva had met with him in his office after she'd closed down the switchboard at five o'clock yesterday.

Princeton tried to make more sense of her discussion with him. Apparently, she'd gotten a little more involved in her research on PPK than he'd anticipated. What he thought was a simple research report was quickly turning into investigative reporting.

The newspaper articles concerned the incidents involving PPK's three major clients - CorpAir, Cygnificant Cruises and Proxential Pharmaceutical. Adiva had shared with him her belief that the mishaps were not accidents, but deliberate. Princeton, of course, found her theory *implausible*, to say the least. Because to give any significant weight to her assertion would inevitably open the door to an even more astonishing question - *who* was the perpetrator?

Adiva Roberts had already answered that question as well.

Princeton had spent much of last night pondering their discussion. And he was still trying to come to terms with it. Could Harvard Prophet actually be that cold and calculating? Surely no account was worth risking the lives of innocent people. He realized that the old man was a bit eccentric and that he'd practically built his life around PPK, but would he go so far as to commit murder to try and sustain what he'd built over the years? It was pretty clear that Harvard stood to lose a lot if CorpAir or any of their major clients walked away.

He scratched his head as he plopped his Nike sneakers on top of his desk. He wanted to chalk this all up to just a figment of Adiva Roberts' imagination. After all, he did recall her saying during their interview that she had a *creative flair* when it came to writing. Was she simply trying to embellish her school report? Princeton glanced at the newspaper articles again. He realized that she was on to something. Adiva didn't create those headlines he was staring at. Those were facts.

Ironically, at the time of their occurrences, he really didn't give any thought to the incidents possibly being connected to the reviews that were in progress. Actually, it would have been absurd to even consider that possibility. Yet, it appeared to have been just that - a very real and distinct correlation. And it had been amazingly effective.

Who would've thought of disrupting an agency review by deliberately creating chaos or a major incident for the client? Sadly, it was a brilliant idea. And Harvard Prophet was a brilliant man.

Adiva had shared with him her belief that Harvard's obsession with growing the ad agency, his pride in having never lost a client, and his own admission that he did not *allow clients to leave his agency,* were all factors that would have motivated him to perpetrate the various mishaps in an effort to thwart or at least disrupt the account review process.

Princeton closed his eyes and tried to absorb it all.

Adiva was a bright girl. She was absolutely certain that she was on the right track. And if she is, then the question that looms is when will an incident occur to stop or disrupt this current review? And more so, how damaging of an incident was Harvard planning?

Princeton realized that he couldn't confront Harvard on this matter. At least not without some hard proof. He wasn't even comfortable discussing it with Duke Priest at the moment. He was just glad that he was able to convince Adiva to keep their discussion between the two of them while they tried to uncover more sustainable evidence.

However, they both realized that time was something that they needed a lot of, and it was the one thing eluding them with each passing day – or hour.

Princeton noticed the time on his watch. This Tuesday seemed to be moving faster than yesterday had. It was lunchtime. But food was the last thing on his mind. He needed a drink – badly.

He double-checked his office door to make certain that it was locked. He had another creative meeting later this afternoon. And he hadn't even prepared for it. The preparations would have to wait. Right now Princeton King was officially on his lunch break. He had another official meeting to attend - his meeting with *Mr. Bud Light*!

Hannah had chosen to ride with Adiva. Partly because She drove a two-seater BMW and she did not want to appear to be showing off. But mainly because driving in Atlanta made her noticeably nervous.

From the moment Adiva turned her snow-white Toyota Corolla onto the private road that led to a circular driveway in front of the multi-million dollar *Prophet Palace,* her eyes grew wide with amazement.

She'd never seen anything so magnificent. She tried to keep herself from staring and gawking at a row of luscious-green magnolia trees that were neatly lined, like officers in the military, along both sides of the circular driveway. And although she wanted to comment on the perfectly manicured hedges they passed as the car came to rest directly in front of the massive estate, she held her tongue.

Hannah was expecting Sebastian to greet them at the door. But the double wooden doors to the entrance of the home were closed. Hannah took hold of the shiny brass knob on the right-side door and turned it. The door opened with ease.

As the two of them entered the huge foyer with its marble flooring, Sebastian suddenly appeared from around a corner. He was a rotund fellow with a full-face beard. Even his head was round. And despite the mound of facial hair, his pouchy chipmunk cheeks were easily discernable. Adiva guessed that he was probably in his mid to upper forties. He greeted them both with a bear hug. His embrace of Hannah lingered just a little while longer.

Sebastian suggested to Hannah that she give Adiva the grand tour while he put the finishing touches on their lunch in his gourmet kitchen. They both agreed that this was a good idea. Hannah instructed Sebastian to bring their lunch into the library when it was ready. She explained to him that Adiva was working on a school report about PPK and that they would be doing some research after their lunch. Adiva wondered where Hannah got the *they*.

The Prophet Palace had been constructed on approximately ten acres of land. The 40,000-square-foot Italian Renaissance estate contained eight bedrooms and ten bathrooms, including a master bedroom that measured 3,200-square-feet alone. There were soaring ceilings and massive moldings throughout the luxurious abode. And other than Sebastian, there were no maids or servants. Hannah explained that her father was a very private man. A cleaning crew came in as necessary to take care of household tasks. Likewise, a grounds crew did the same for the landscaping chores. Sebastian lived in the carriage house that was directly across from the six-car garage.

After a tour of the downstairs area, Hannah wasn't able to take Adiva on a tour of the upstairs because Sebastian had announced that their lunch was served. The two women sat down at a large, round, cherry wood table that was positioned in the center of the library.

The library was enormous. Wood-paneled bookshelves that stretched from the floor to the ceiling lined the walls. It also contained a hidden staircase that led directly to Harvard Prophet's master bedroom. Adiva speculated that the mansion had to be worth millions. If this home was the result of a successful career in advertising, she was glad that she'd chosen this field.

It took less than forty-five minutes for them to devour their lunch. Adiva was now too tired to work. Although she realized that she should get started. She figured that this library probably contained just about everything the one at the office did. Volumes of books, neatly arranged according to Harvard's personal preference, left no vacancies on the shelves. There was a special collection on the PPK agency as well.

Hannah told Adiva to feel free to look through whatever materials she wanted. She told her that she needed to go upstairs and make a phone call and that she would join her shortly. Adiva assumed that Hannah was probably going to her room to call her *friend* – Radford Albright in London.

After Hannah's departure from the library, Adiva stared at the rows and rows of books. She realized that she didn't have time to stand and goggle. She needed to peruse as many files as she could within the limited time left before they returned to the office. She was especially hoping to find *anything* that could support her theory.

She spotted a wooden antique-looking two-drawer file tucked away in a corner of the library. When she tried to open the top drawer it was locked. She tried the second drawer. It was also locked.

As she wandered about the quiet, cozy room, her roving eyes came to rest on an expensive-looking oil painting. It was a Picasso. Although its identity was unbeknownst to her.

It was probably glued to the wall, she thought to herself. And to test her hypothesis, Adiva attempted to lift the painting by taking hold of the bottom portion of the frame. The painting moved with ease. It wasn't glued to the wall after all.

However, just behind the painting, Adiva noticed a tiny black button that was recessed into the wall. Without any hesitation she lifted the painting slightly with her left arm while using her right thumb to depress the black button.

She was startled by a motorized hum as the wall slid slowly to the right, revealing a curved staircase.

This must be the hidden staircase that Hannah mentioned to her. Again, absent of any hesitation, Adiva ascended the stairs. The top of the staircase yielded large French doors. Adiva reached out her hand and turned the shiny brass handle. The door opened almost effortlessly. Her eyes bulged in wonderment as she stepped into the room. Her mouth dropped slightly. This was far from the average bedroom. There were Oriental rugs delicately stationed in various locales on the polished hardwood floor. The huge bed itself was splendidly adorned in Irish linen that was lined with Indian silk. A sofa, covered with herringbone-textured chenille, sat adjacent from the bed. The windows were draped in fabric featuring an English leaf design.

Adiva was completely astonished at the room's opulence.

She then made her way into Harvard's bathroom. Once there, she was equally impressed. This must truly be his oasis, she mumbled to herself. Everything within the bathroom - from the diagonal sink wall to the built-in bench inside the shower stall, created an atmosphere of pure richness and harmony.

As Adiva prepared to exit the bathroom, something caught her eye. It was a bath towel that was left draped over the limestone counter top. It wasn't so much the white towel that sparked her interest, but rather the large initials that were imprinted in black lettering on the towel. They read *S.B.* Adiva wondered whose initials they were.

Certainly not Harvard's or Hannah's. Sebastian was also ruled out - his last name was *Lauterbach.* Hannah had told her that he was from Germany.

"What are you doing in here?"

Adiva emitted a faint scream. "Girl, you scared me!" she yelled at Hannah. Although she realized that at the moment she had no plausible explanation for why she was in Hannah's father's bathroom.

"Sorry. I didn't mean to frighten you. But I've been looking all over for you. How did you get in here?"

Adiva's heartbeat hadn't quite returned to normal. "Uh, well, I guess I sort of wandered in," she began explaining. "I mean, while I was in the library I accidentally discovered this button which, when I pressed it caused the wall to slide away. I then saw these stairs, so I climbed them and eventually ended up here."

The expression on Hannah's face was obvious disbelief. "The button that opens the wall is *hidden,* Adiva. You couldn't just *accidentally* find it. You had to be looking for it," Hannah discoursed.

Adiva didn't like what she was alluding to. "I wasn't looking for anything, Hannah. I admit that I was curious about the painting on the wall, which is how I discovered the button."

"Yes, but you'd have to actually lift or remove the painting in order to see the button. Were you trying to *remove* the painting from the wall?"

Adiva became quite defensive. "Are you accusing me of trying to steal your father's painting?"

Hannah didn't respond.

"Well, I wasn't. And I resent your insinuation! My god, what did you expect me to do? Hide that big ol' painting beneath my skirt?"

"Adiva, I'm not accusing you of anything. But that is a very expensive painting. It's worth thousands of dollars. Daddy bought – "

"I don't care what it's worth!" Adiva shouted, interrupting her. "I consider myself a Christian and I've never stolen anything in my life! I may not have millions of dollars in my bank account, Hannah Prophet, but what I do have I've earned every cent!"

"Adiva, dahling," Hannah attempted to appease her. "All I was trying to say was that, in order for *anybody* to find the button to open the wall, the painting would have to have been removed. I mean, I just asked a question, that was all."

"No you didn't, Hannah. All you did was accuse me of trying to steal and I resent your accusation."

"All right, all right. If you think that's what I was doing, then I'm sorry. It's just that, well, when I asked you what you were doing in here you looked like tail lights trapped on a deer."

Adiva hesitated before responding – trying her best not to laugh at this girl's repeated incorrect use of clichés. "Girl, you mean *a deer caught in headlights.*"

"Of course," Hannah replied. "Well, we'd better be going. If daddy ever found out that you located his hidden staircase, or that you were in his bedroom . . . well, you'd just better make sure that he never finds out!"

You don't have to worry about me telling him, Adiva thought to herself.

The two women returned to the library before leaving the mansion to make certain that the wall had been re-closed. Adiva was disappointed that she hadn't obtained any additional information. Although she was glad that she came. If she had any hopes of getting Hannah to cooperate at some point, she would have to strengthen their friendship as much as possible.

CHAPTER SEVENTEEN

HARVARD PROPHET'S SMILE WAS venomous as he meticulously slid the video tape into a plain brown envelope. He'd decided that it was time to alert the Missus to Princeton King's drinking antics. He figured that by doing so it would perhaps create enough havoc between the two of them to keep Princeton away from the agency for a while.

Princeton had been drinking so much lately that Harvard found him to be of no use to the CorpAir review or to the agency as a whole. And he didn't particularly want him screwing things up - not at this critical stage.

He would be more than willing to keep the idiot around if he was really worried about the review. But he wasn't. He was certain that if all goes well this review should come screeching to a halt very soon.

Harvard's secretary was out of the office today so he strolled down the corridor - in his familiar cool and hip manner - toward the receptionist area. He'd have to get Miss Roberts to handle this package for him.

Adiva was surprised to see Harvard standing in front of her counter. She rarely seen him around the office and she definitely had little, if any, dialogue with him because his calls were sent directly to his personal secretary who would screen them before transferring them to his office.

"Good afternoon, Mr. Prophet," she greeted him, politely.

Harvard made an obligatory nod. "Miss Roberts."

"I didn't know that you were coming out here because I just sent a call to your office," she informed him. While his secretary was out, Adiva had been instructed to send his calls directly to him.

He quickly dismissed it as being no big deal. "It will go to my voice mail." He then glanced around the reception area – his eyes darting back and forth.

"Is there something wrong?" Adiva asked.

He chose not to answer her. "Here," he said, reaching across the counter to hand her the brown envelope, after he was certain that no one else was nearby. "See to it that a courier picks this up immediately and deliver it to Princeton King's home," he instructed her. "Address it to Muriel – his wife."

Adiva jotted down his instructions on a nearby Post-It note. "I'll take care of it right away," she replied, not giving any thought to the request, the envelope itself nor its contents.

Back at his office, Harvard closed the door and locked it. He shuffled over to his desk and exhaled a soft grunt as he sat down in the chair. Aging was hell. His reading glasses lay on his desk. He retrieved them and proceeded to look up the phone number for

Philip Hetzler in a small phone directory that he kept inside of his desk drawer.

As the phone on the other end began to ring, Harvard peeked at his watch – not even three o'clock yet – he should still be around. It wasn't as if the doctor had many patients to see, he chuckled to himself.

"Dr. Hetzler here," he answered.

"Why Phil – it's such a shame that you now have to answer your own telephone," Harvard grinned. He enjoyed teasing him.

"What do you want?"

Harvard's facetious grin evaporated. "You know damn well what I want!" he snapped. "My patience has run dry, Phil!"

Dr. Hetzler could feel his stomach starting to churn. He realized that he'd made no headway in trying to persuade Duke Priest to sell his fifteen-percent share of the ad agency.

"Harvard, I cannot rush this matter along any faster than I already am," he told him.

There was a moment of silence. "I'm beginning to think that you're not going to be able to fulfill your end of the deal," Harvard began, his voice tinged with menace.

On the other end of the phone, Dr. Hetzler gripped the phone tighter, a pained expression settling on his face. "I, uh – I told you that I would make it happen," his words were miserably unconvincing.

"I am not a man who is accustomed to losing, Phil," Harvard's voice grew maniacal. "I simply will not allow it!"

"Are you threatening me?"

Harvard laughed out loud. "Surely you jest, Phil! Threats are idle words as far as I'm concerned."

Another moment of silence.

"What I want and what I expect from you, doctor, is exactly what I've been paying you for!" Harvard shouted this time. "Give me my damn completed transaction or else!" He slammed the phone onto its console with an angry force. And no sooner had he done so, the phone rang. He pressed the intercom button. "What!"

"Excuse me, Mr. Prophet," came Adiva's soft voice through the intercom.

"What is it, Miss Roberts?"

"I have a gentleman on the line who is insisting that he speak with you. He says it's personal and confidential."

"What gentleman?"

"A *Mr. Goodwin Young.*"

Harvard was surprised. Goodwin Young was the co-founder and chairman of the billion-dollar New York ad agency Young & Lucas. They were also one of the two agencies scheduled to pitch CorpAir in the final round of presentations next month.

"You may put him through," Harvard gave her the okay.

"Thank you," Adiva replied as she transferred the call to his office.

"Goodwin!" Harvard bellowed his name when the call came through to him. "I must say I wasn't expecting to hear from my arch rival on this fine afternoon!"

Goodwin Young began a staccato laugh. "And just how are you doing, Harvard?"

"I couldn't be better!"

"Great. Just Great."

"What's on your mind, Goodwin?"

"Well, I am going to be in Atlanta this evening and I wondered if you might join me for dinner?"

What could he possibly be up to, Harvard thought to himself. "What's the occasion?"

"Oh, I'd rather not get into it over the phone. But suffice it to say, the meeting might prove mutually beneficial."

Harvard took a quick glance at his desk calendar, which lay in front of him. "What time are we talking?"

"I've got an eight o'clock reservation - will that work for you?"

"Of course. Eight o'clock will be fine. I have some other business matters to address prior to that time, but I don't anticipate a problem."

Goodwin Young was delighted. "Splendid! The restaurant is a fairly new establishment down there - on the north side of town - " he paused as he flipped through some notes. "—Ah yes, here it is. The *SilverFish.* Are you familiar with the place?"

"Absolutely," Harvard answered. "They serve some of the best seafood that I've ever eaten."

"Well, that's good to hear. The place came highly recommended from a colleague of mine. I look forward to the dining experience."

The two agency rivals chatted briefly before terminating their call. Neither of them had made any reference to the CorpAir account review.

Harvard dialed his daughter's extension. When she answered he got right to the point and explained to her that he would have to cancel their father/daughter Tuesday night out at the movies. Hannah was deeply disappointed, though she tried to hide it from him. It was something that she'd become an expert at doing over the years.

Duke Priest waited patiently and alone in a small booth at the over-crowded café on Lenox Road. He checked his watch again for the umpteenth time. It was almost 7:30. Dr. Hetzler had asked to meet him at the café at 7:00.

An attractive young waitress came by the booth and poured more hot coffee into Duke's near-empty white porcelain cup. He smiled and thanked her politely. She inquired again as to whether or not someone else would be joining him. Duke assured her that his guest would be arriving very soon. She cast him a frustrated look, as if he were detaining her from something much more important. Finally, and obviously not satisfied with his answer, her eyes gave him a peremptory gesture as she strutted away.

Duke's eyes searched the front of the café hoping to see Dr. Hetzler coming through the door. It was soon 7:45. Duke decided that he was going to leave. Just as he stood from the table, Dr. Hetzler rushed to the booth. He apologized munificently while stating that his tardiness couldn't be helped. A different waitress came to their table and brought coffee to Dr. Hetzler before she scribbled their dinner order on a tiny white note pad.

"I really appreciate you meeting me here on such short notice," Dr. Hetzler said.

"It sounded urgent," Duke replied.

"I suppose you could say that it is. I hope that I'm not keeping you from some other engagement for the evening?" Dr. Hetzler thought it was only appropriate that he ask the question. Although, he was fully aware that any social activities within Duke's life barely existed.

"It's all right, Phil. I am curious, however, why we couldn't just meet at your office?"

Dr. Hetzler began to fidget. "Well, that's part of the reason why I called this meeting."

"I don't quite follow," Duke said, puzzled.

"Duke, if you would, allow me to be candid with you."

Duke nodded in agreement.

"You see, I closed my practice today."

Duke had already begun to guide the steaming coffee cup to his lips. His body eagerly awaited the rich brew to penetrate through his anatomy. But the white porcelain cup never made it to his lips. Slowly, he returned the cup to its matching saucer. "You did what?"

"I'm done with it. Finished. And it's been a long time coming."

"What brought all of this on?"

"Well, first I must explain everything to you."

Duke leaned his body forward. "I'm listening."

Dr. Hetzler found it difficult to look Duke in the eye. "I have an eleven o'clock flight to Portland, Maine tomorrow night. It's my home. I'm returning there to live and to teach."

"Phil – forgive the reference – but are you out of your mind! I mean you don't go from having a thriving practice one day to closing up shop the next! What's come over you?"

"That's just it, Duke. The practice isn't thriving. In fact, it hasn't been for quite some time. I intended to close it several months ago – that is, until I met this gentleman. Or more accurately, he found me."

"What gentleman?"

Dr. Hetzler allowed a deep sigh to escape. "Harvard Prophet."

"Harvard? Are we talking about the same Harvard Prophet? What does he have to do with any of this?" Duke's voice was raised.

Another deep sigh from Dr. Hetzler.

"Calm down, Duke . . . "

"Don't assume that I'm upset!" Duke interrupted him. "Not yet anyway."

Dr. Hetzler apologized for making the assumption. He assured Duke that he was going to explain everything to him. However, he did not want to be repeatedly interrupted. Duke agreed to allow him to fully explain what was going on.

Dr. Hetzler averted his eyes from Duke and began to stare into his coffee cup. He slowly stirred cream into the dark liquid until it was a caramel color. He knew what needed to be said. But knowing it and actually saying it had created an impasse. There was a bit of irony to this meeting. For once, it was he who felt as if he were a patient. He could actually say now that he knew what it must feel like for patients to try and free the truth from their hearts. It was a dilemma that he'd witnessed many of his patients wrestle with throughout his years of practicing psychiatry. Very few of them could ever just open up and tell him exactly what was on their minds without him constantly prodding and probing them. Now, he found himself beating around the bush. He began to question himself as to what he hoped to accomplish by meeting with Duke. Hadn't the damage already been done?

"Are you okay, Phil?"

Dr. Hetzler cleared his throat several times as he usually did and then he forced a couple of coughs. "Of course, I'm fine," he answered. "Just trying to gather my thoughts."

Realizing that he'd stalled long enough, Dr. Hetzler began to explain to Duke how he initially received a telephone call at his office several months ago from Harvard Prophet. Harvard had insisted on meeting with him. When he tried to question the nature of the meeting, Harvard declined to discuss matters over the phone. He only told him that it concerned one of his patients. A meeting was then scheduled for later that evening at Dr. Hetzler's office.

It was during that meeting that Dr. Hetzler learned of Harvard's diabolical intentions. Harvard attempted to convince Dr. Hetzler that it was in Duke's best interest if he sold his fifteen-percent stake in the agency. He explained how the pressures of being a partner in the agency had taken its toll on Duke's emotional health. Harvard had even made up some rather convincing examples of how the agency was being negatively affected.

Dr. Hetzler was able to see right through Harvard's propaganda. Although he didn't know the man prior, he had read about him many times in the press. He knew the man was overly ambitious. But once Harvard began to discuss monetary payments in return for inducing Duke to sell, Dr. Hetzler had found himself being drawn more into Harvard's web of deceit. After all, his practice had run into some very serious financial difficulties. In fact, most of his patients at that time had all but dissipated. And before he realized it, Dr. Hetzler had rationalized his involvement in Harvard's scheme to the point where he'd convinced himself that Duke's emotional stability *was* at stake.

As Dr. Hetzler continued to reveal the sordid truth, Duke sat motionless across from him. He face void of expression. He never really cared much for Harvard Prophet, but he'd made every attempt to show respect for him as a business partner. He was even quick to excuse much of Harvard's eccentric behavior as nothing more than his preoccupation with being in the limelight. Out in front.

Duke was not going to pity Harvard Prophet, though he felt it was sad for him to stoop to such a level as he did. It was Phil whom he felt sorry for. Duke was very much aware of how influential and demanding Harvard could be when there was something that he wanted. Phil had simply been vulnerable. And Harvard knew all too well how to pounce on someone else's vulnerability.

"I would fully understand it if you chose to report me to the medical board, or even if you chose to sue me," Dr. Hetzler said solemnly.

Duke removed his horn-rimmed eyeglasses and began to wipe them with one of the table napkins. "That thought never crossed my mind, Phil.

"However, I can't say that I'm not unsettled by all of this."

"Of course."

"Oddly enough, I understand that you did what you felt you had to do under the circumstances - we're all forced to do that sometimes."

"That's a bunch of crap, Duke! You were my patient, for god sake! I compromised my professional ethics as well as my moral values. I saw an opportunity and in one giant step I crossed the line on doctor-patient confidentiality! How can you possibly say that you *understand* what I did? My actions are incomprehensible!"

"Because I know *the man*!" Duke shouted. "I've worked with him for the past ten years. He's been after my fifteen-percent share of PPK from day one. If he hadn't found you to use as a pawn, Phil, he would have eventually found someone else! Harvard will stop at nothing to get what he wants."

Dr. Hetzler allowed his head to drop. He closed his eyes and wrestled intensely with his own emotions. Looking Duke in the eyes had become overwhelmingly difficult. To say that he was ashamed would be grossly understating how he felt at the moment. He was more than ashamed. He was beyond disgraced. Philip James Hetzler felt lower than the worst scum.

The waitress appeared with their dinner. Both men ate in silence. Dr. Hetzler kept his moistening eyes focused on his plate. The silence between them was so keen that only the swallowing of their food was audible. Occasionally, Dr. Hetzler would remove his handkerchief from his back pocket to dry his eyes. He couldn't prevent the tears from continually welling up.

Duke appeared deep in thought.

"I'm curious, what was the big payoff for finally getting me to agree to sell?" Duke asked him.

Dr. Hetzler finally allowed his eyes to confront his patient - the innocent victim. "I was suppose to receive a final cash payment of $150,000," he answered.

Duke shook his head in disbelief. "So, I take it Harvard still thinks that I'm going to sell to him?"

Dr. Hetzler nodded yes.

"Have you told him that you've closed your practice?"

"No. I haven't discussed it with anyone other than my wife and you."

"What does your wife have to say about it?"

"She knows nothing of my arrangement with Harvard. However, she is aware of my financial problems with the practice. She fully supports my decision to move back to Portland. You know, to start over."

"There's got to be a better way around this, Phil?"

"I wish there was. But no, I don't think that I have the heart, never mind the audacity, to counsel another patient after what I've succumb to."

"Well, if it's any comfort to you, Phil, I forgive you for what you did."

The words must have been the latch to unlock the gate on Dr. Hetzler's attempt to restrain his emotions because his eyes over-flowed with tears and he began to weep openly. Duke didn't quite know whether to embrace him, pat him on the back or simply allow him to rid himself of the bitter tears. Finally, he stretched his arm across the table and laid his hand on Dr. Hetzler's shoulder.

"It's all right, Phil," he whispered. "It's all right."

Once Dr. Hetzler had regained his composure, Duke shared with him a plan that he'd come up with while sitting there. Duke explained that it was a plan of retribution for both he and Dr. Hetzler. After hearing it, Dr. Hetzler was in full support of it. They both chuckled as they reviewed the details of the plan again.

The two men passed on desserts, choosing instead to call it an evening. Duke joked with Dr. Hetzler by asking if he was being billed for their time. "No, Duke. This one's on the house!" he answered in between laughs as they exited the café.

Goodwin Young had eaten at many of New York City's finest restaurants. He could literally smell the good ones from the bad ones before he ever entered their doors. When he exited the shiny black limousine in front of the SilverFish restaurant, just north of Atlanta, he knew that a palatable dinner awaited him.

Goodwin was an accomplished advertising industry veteran. His compact frame lacked the muscular build of Harvard's. Yet, his body had been well maintained for his sixty-eight years. His oval-shaped head was matted with dove gray hair. And his *Clark Gable* mustache failed to augment his withered complexion.

Harvard was already seated at a large, round table that was draped in a white linen tablecloth. Two, dark blue, leather winged back chairs were positioned on each side of the table. The table was carefully adorned with white and gold trimmed plates, two gold-finished forks and a knife. White linen napkins were also adorning the table. The napkins had been shaped into the form of a fish.

The menu at the SilverFish was both comprehensive and exhaustive. But the tantalizing read was worth every delicate description - from the sizzling appetizers like Clams Cilantro and Cinnamon Calamari, to more inspiring dishes like the Southern Seafood Salad - a succulent meat combination of lobster, shrimp and salmon; further enhanced with sautéed spinach and served with the customer's choice of Burgundies.

The crisply clad waiters and waitresses moved about the spacious restaurant like graceful dancers as live classical music guided them to their various stations.

"Have you been waiting long?" Goodwin Young asked Harvard, as he took a seat at the table.

"Actually, I just arrived not more than five minutes ago," Harvard answered, glancing at his Piaget.

"Great."

Both men began perusing the menu. The waiter arrived at the table and asked if he could get them anything to drink. Harvard ordered a red wine and Goodwin settled for Chardonnay.

"I suppose you're anxious to find out why I asked to meet with you," Goodwin began.

Harvard improvised a smile. "My interest has been piqued."

"Well, I won't keep you in suspense any longer." Goodwin sipped the Chardonnay that had just been set before him. "I'd like for you to consider an acquisition," he said forthrightly.

"An acquisition of what?" Harvard asked, sincerely.

"Young and Lucas acquiring Prophet, Priest and King, of course."

"You must be kidding?"

"I've never been more serious, Harvard."

Harvard raised his glass of red wine to his lips and then drank a long sip. He swallowed hard. "I've never had any desire to sell or merge my agency, Goodwin. Surely you know that."

"Times change. Feelings change. The whole landscape is about to change, Harvard."

"If this is the reason for your inviting me to dinner, Goodwin, then I'm sorry to say, but it has indeed been an utter waste of time - mine as well as yours."

Goodwin was prepared for Harvard's reaction. "Just hear me out," he pressed.

Harvard didn't commit himself with an answer. He allowed his silence to indicate his willingness to at least hear what Goodwin had to say.

Goodwin acted on the passive gesture. "I think that you'll agree, Harvard, that Y&L is poised to win CorpAir."

Harvard stiffened at his effrontery, but kept silent.

"With that fact in mind, PPK stands to lose at least half of its billings - provided none of your other four accounts choose to walk as well. And - "

Harvard interrupted, "We have every intention of maintaining CorpAir on our roster."

"Intentions are well and good, Harvard. But you and I both know that *good intentions* do not win accounts in this business."

"So, have you totally eliminated Graystone from the mix?" Harvard asked, referring to the other New York agency contending for the CorpAir account.

Goodwin flashed an animated smile. "C'mon now, Harvard. Graystone never had a chance in this review."

"What I don't quite understand, Goodwin, is this – if you're so damn sure that Y&L has CorpAir all sewn up, then why in the hell do you need to acquire PPK?"

"Synergies," he answered, matter-of-factly. "Pure and simple. PPK would fit nicely under our umbrella."

"Well, I'm not quite convinced that you have CorpAir in your bag as yet."

Goodwin waited a moment while the waiter refilled his Chardonnay. "Harvard, who do you think is behind the pending alliance between CorpAir and EuroAir? Y&L has been putting this relationship together for quite some time. CorpAir desperately needs an alliance with an international partner. EuroAir is the perfect match. And Y&L is the glue that's cementing the two of them."

Harvard downed more of his wine. "Sorry to disappoint you, Goodwin. But my agency is not for sale." He pushed his chair away from the table and stood.

"There's no reason to leave, Harvard. Dinner hasn't even been served."

Harvard fanned the air with his hands to show his dissent. "Frankly, I've lost my appetite." He then reached into the inside breast pocket of his suit jacket and retrieved his wallet. He placed a $100 bill onto the table. "This should cover the wine."

As he turned from the table to leave the place, Goodwin called out to him. Harvard turned and faced him. "I'm going to enjoy snatching CorpAir away from you," he said, flashing a superior smile.

"Not in this lifetime!" Harvard responded, and then strolled away.

CHAPTER EIGHTEEN

A CRICK HAD DEVELOPED IN HER NECK during the more than two hours that she spent curled under the desk of Harvard Prophet. At first, Adiva Roberts hid in the ladies' restroom after five o'clock. Once the cleaning crew began to make their rounds, she slipped from the restroom. She'd watched Harvard leave around seven o'clock. And when someone from the cleaning crew unlocked his office around 8:15, she waited down the corridor for an opportunity to dash inside. She was almost discovered crouched beneath the desk as an elderly man began to vacuum Harvard's office. Her tiny body was still practically squashed under the massive desk's less than massive opening.

When Adiva was certain that the cleaning crew had gone, she crawled out. She used both of her hands to massage her aching neck. It was almost 10:30. She knew that she had to hurry. She'd spoken to Granny Rae earlier and explained to her that she would be working late at the GSU library. She hated lying to her grandmother, but it couldn't be helped.

Adiva opened her purse and removed a small flashlight the size of a pen. She'd bought the device at a gadget shop in the mall. She decided that it was better not to turn on the lights. She also remained on her knees as she moved about the office. First, she checked the door to make certain that it was locked. Then she crawled back to Harvard's desk and initiated her search there. She went through each of the desk drawers except the bottom right-hand drawer. It was locked. Adiva didn't give up.

She removed a fingernail file from her purse and inserted it into the drawer's lock. Carefully, she prodded and wiggled the tip of the fingernail file inside the drawer's lock. This technique always seemed to work in the movies, she thought to herself.

It wasn't long before she heard a slight click and the drawer slid open. She held the flashlight over the drawer so that she could read the top of the file folders that appeared to be neatly arranged. Adiva had gotten all the way to the back of the drawer when she saw the red file folder. Printed across the tab of the folder were the words MISHAPS. Her heart almost skipped a beat.

Adiva pulled the folder from the drawer. When she opened it she counted three original newspaper articles. They had been folded twice in order to fit snugly into the letter-size folder. The newsprint had begun to fade on the two earlier articles. She quickly removed them. They were the same ones that she'd copied from microfiche at the library last weekend.

She wasn't sure if she should take the entire file. She realized that having the original articles in her possession could be beneficial. She decided not to take them. She placed the folder back into the drawer and closed it. She was relieved when she tried to pull on the drawer and found that it had locked itself again. Adiva then replaced the fingernail file back inside her purse.

Adiva stood and hunkered over Harvard's desk. She allowed the flashlight to scan the calendar on his desk. He had the date of *Friday, July 25th* circled in a black marking. And written beneath the date were the words *D-Day*! She made a note of the date as well as the words on a piece of paper and stuffed it into her purse.

Adiva began a slow crawl toward the door when she heard footsteps. She froze. Then she heard someone fumbling with his or her keys. She realized that it must be Harvard. She tried to think quickly. She didn't want to go back under the desk because she was certain that he would be sitting down there. When she heard the key being inserted into the doorknob she stood quickly and scampered across the large office where she took cover between the sofa and an end table. Her heart was pounding faster than a jackhammer in her ears.

The door opened and Harvard stepped inside, flipping on the light switch. She reacted to the sudden brightness of the room by squinting her eyes.

What was he doing here at this time of the night? If she gets caught how would she even begin to explain her presence in his office?

Gingerly, Adiva peeked from behind the sofa. She was bent so low that her back began to ache in addition to her sore neck. Harvard was standing in front of his desk with his reading glasses hanging from his nose. He was examining a file from the brass tray atop his desk. He quickly closed the file and replaced it in the tray again and began walking toward the sofa.

Adiva jerked her head back behind the sofa. Fear had consumed her entire body. What was she going to do? If Harvard Prophet found her there would be no way that she could explain her actions. She was absolutely convinced that he was a ruthless individual. What would he do to her? Firing her would be too easy. The man was crazy.

Adiva shut her eyes and prayed as the footsteps drew closer and then stopped. What was he doing now? She peeked again from behind the sofa. She watched as Harvard removed a painting from the wall. She could see that the painting looked exactly like the one she'd seen earlier today in the library at the Prophet Palace.

He pressed the button that the painting concealed. And just like in the library earlier, there was a slight motorized humming sound as the wall slid open. Adiva could see that it was some sort of a room. But she couldn't see what was inside the room.

She listened intently as Harvard stepped inside the room. She could hear clicking noises. Harvard had begun to review the tape of Adiva's visit with Princeton King yesterday evening. He increased the volume. Adiva was shocked when she heard her own voice conversing with Princeton.

Oh my god, she thought. The entire office must be bugged. If he heard their conversation from yesterday then that means he was on to her. Then why hadn't he confronted her? She recalled her brief encounter with him this afternoon when he brought her the package to have delivered to Princeton's wife. What was that all about? She hadn't given any thought to it before now.

She continued to listen as Harvard listened to the conversation where Adiva was explaining her theory. How that she felt he was behind all of the mishaps.

For the first time, Adiva began to regret her decision to pursue this inquisition. Why didn't she leave well enough alone? Harvard was a very powerful man. If he was responsible for what she thought he was, Adiva realized that her own life might be in danger.

Her thoughts turned to Granny Rae. If something happened to her who would take care of Granny Rae? Adiva had no siblings and Granny Rae had no other family members – at least none that she was aware of. And what would happen to Soupa Mann? Who would be there to help him correct the error of his ways? That is exactly what she should have been doing – trying to mend fences with Soupa

Mann; instead she was crouched behind this sofa in this office building playing the role of *Nancy Drew*.

The audiotape finally stopped. Adiva heard Harvard mumbling, but she couldn't make out what it was he was saying. She continued to watch as he stepped from the secret room. The wall was re-closed and the painting placed back onto the wall to conceal the little button.

Hastily, Harvard grabbed his keys from the desk. He flipped the lights off and walked out of the office. Adiva breathed a sigh of relief when she heard the door being locked. But she remained behind the sofa for at least fifteen minutes after he'd left the office. She wanted to be sure that he was out of the building.

Finally, she stood and stretched. Her body ached horrendously. She began to shake each of her legs to try and regain the feeling in them. Once her heartbeat had returned to its normal rhythm, Adiva quickly made her way to the door and exited.

As she got off the elevator and entered the lobby, she nearly ran toward the main exit doors. The loud voice of a security guard stopped her.

"Excuse me, Miss?"

Adiva's heart began pounding again. Slowly, she turned around. "Yes," she answered, trying not to appear nervous.

"I'll need for you to sign out, please," he said. "Anyone leaving the building after seven o'clock must sign out," he explained.

"Uh, sure. I forgot," she lied again, for the second time today. She'd never worked beyond seven o'clock before so she wasn't familiar with this rule. She took hold of the pen, which was constrained by a long silver chain to the security guard's desk. She glanced at her watch and entered the time of *11:10 p.m.* into the sign-out book, which lay opened.

However, before signing her name in the *signature* field of the book, Adiva hesitated briefly. Then she very neatly signed her name *Nancy Drew* and hurried from the building.

◈◈◈◈◈◈◈

Princeton King was slouched on the sofa in his den. It was almost midnight and he'd been drinking beers since he came home just after six and found the letter attached to the refrigerator's door.

Muriel and the kids were gone.

He phoned her parent's home in Chicago but there was no answer. It didn't make sense to him how she found out - but she had. He'd spoken to his wife around two o'clock this afternoon and she gave him no indication that she knew about his drinking nor that she was leaving. He realized that she must have left suddenly because she barely took any of her clothes and most the kids' things were also left behind.

Princeton's right hand held the neatly written one page letter. It was now crumpled into a ball. He adjusted his posture on the sofa and began to unravel the letter. He switched on a nearby lamp, quickly illuminating the room. He'd been sitting in the dark for the past several hours. He used the back of his hand and rubbed his bloodshot eyes. His head had started to ache. A dull expression blanketed his face as he read the letter again:

It's over Prince. I won't live with your lies anymore, and I won't allow the kids to be exposed to this. I know all about your drinking at the office. Save yourself the agony of denying it because I now have proof. God only knows how long you've been lying to me and to our family. You can have the house – I don't want it. I'll send for the rest of my things later. You can handle the dissolution of the marriage however you choose. I won't contest it. And I'm not asking anything from you. I know you'll do right by the kids. I do want sole custody, Prince. I won't compromise where the kids are concerned. I truly wished that I could have been stronger for you. I tried Prince – I really did try. But it's just too difficult. I realize that there are things that we'll need to discuss. But not right now. Please give the kids and I time to adjust. I wish the best for you.

Love, Muriel.

P.S. The kids said goodbye.

Princeton had never felt so alone as he did now. He feared that this day would one day come. He always hoped that it would not. Despite what Muriel had said in the letter, she hadn't tried. She'd given up on their twelve-year marriage long before he started drinking. It was the insurmountable marital problems that led him to the drinking.

His wife had always wanted a way out. Her incessant nagging had failed. So she kept pushing and pushing until she drove him to drinking. And now she was using that against him. It was her excuse to leave. Dismantle the family.

Muriel was a very difficult woman to understand and to please. She seemed happiest when the two of them were being contentious. If there was nothing to argue about she'd invent something.

Princeton berated himself for all the times he allowed himself to be dragged into her web of self-pity and misery. He knew in his heart that if it weren't for the kids he would have walked away years ago. No two people should be this unhappy.

At least one of them was happy now. She was out. She got what she wanted.

Ironically, Muriel had never been all that happy living in Chicago either. Which is why Princeton thought that the move to Atlanta along with the prospect of starting a new agency would have strengthened their relationship. Now, Chicago was the place she was headed back to.

He wasn't surprised by her irrational behavior. He'd gotten used to it.

Princeton tossed the letter aside. It sailed across the den and landed beneath the fireplace mantle. He wasn't going to chase after her. Life was too short for this. Let her be the one to have to explain to Alyson and Nicholas why their father was no longer a regular part of their lives. Of course, he was certain that she'd make up some lies about him. But in the end, the kids would grow to hate *her* not him.

Things happened for a reason. Maybe this was how it was supposed to end. He and Muriel have traveled this road as far as they could. Both of them had seen the warning signs along the way, but they chose to keep on traveling the same road - day in and day out.

They were at a dead end now. And Princeton realized that he simply did not have the energy or the desire to turn around and go back the other way. If this is where the road ended, then so be it. Muriel had voluntarily abandoned the vehicle, not him. The ride had become just too bumpy for her to remain. Never mind the *for better or for worse,* or the *until death do us part.* There was nothing left for him to do now except find another road - a different path.

Getting through this would not be easy by any stretch of the imagination. But he knew that he would get through it - one day at a time.

CHAPTER NINETEEN

HARVARD PROPHET DID NOT LEAVE HIS stately mansion at the usual 6:30 a.m. on this particular morning. Instead, as the six-thirty time ticked away, Harvard continued to sip his café au lait while allowing himself to enjoy the warmth of the July early morning breeze.

He was fully dressed in a double-breasted, navy suit as he sat at the wrought iron table on his veranda. His legs were crossed. And the early morning sunrise reflected quite nicely off his well-polished burgundy loafers. The shoes had been a birthday gift from his daughter a couple of months ago. She'd even had his initials engraved into the heel of each shoe.

This week's edition of Advertising Age magazine lay spread across the table, occupying much of the table space, with just a corner of the table reserved for his cup and saucer.

Harvard simpered as he stared at this week's Ad Age cover story. In a bold headline it was being announced that *General Motors* was placing its *$2.6 billion* media account up for review. GM was indisputably the country's largest advertiser. Their review was going to be the largest account review in ad history.

He shook his head incredulously. He would not want to be the incumbent agency on that account. After he'd finished reading the GM article, Harvard grabbed his cellular phone, which was positioned on the table and covered beneath the pages of the tabloid-size magazine.

"Did I wake you?" he asked when the call was answered on the other end.

"No, I've been awake for an hour now."

"I wanted to apologize for not dropping by last night – a late business meeting precluded me."

"It happens."

"Listen, when this review is completed, I'm going to treat you to a get-away vacation. Where would you like to go?"

"That's very generous of you. But I'm not sure if I can spare the time."

"You'll make the time. It's an order!" he teased.

"You're the boss."

"So, tell me – where will it be?"

"How about the Caribbean? I've always wanted to go the Caribbean!"

"Then the Caribbean it shall be!"

"Will you come along?"

"Of course. Do you think I'm going to allow you to meander along the beaches of the Caribbean without me?"

"I welcome your company."

"Good. It's been quite awhile since we've had an opportunity to celebrate something so grand."

"You're referring to the fact that we're going to keep CorpAir onboard?"

"Most definitely."

"I've always admired your confidence."

Harvard chuckled.

"I guess I don't have anything to worry about, huh?" the caller asked him.

"Worry doesn't become you, sweetheart."

There was a sheepish smile on the other end of the phone.

"I wish that our relationship didn't have to be so secretive."

"We've discussed that a million times already," Harvard sighed. "For now, it has to be this way."

"If you say so."

"Well, I have to run. See you at the office." Harvard immediately clicked the phone off. As he prepared to put the magazine away, Hannah appeared on the veranda.

"Good morning, daddy!" she greeted him, her face exuding cheerfulness. She was still adorned in her bathrobe.

"Well good morning, honey! Did you sleep well last night?"

"I tossed a little," she answered him.

"Something wrong?"

Hannah poked out her bottom lip. This tactic had been used successfully a number of times over the years. "Daddy, I miss you."

"Honey, I haven't gone anywhere. I'm right here."

"I know that. It's just . . . well, we don't spend any time together."

"Hannah, dear, you know that this CorpAir review is consuming an awful lot of my time right now," Harvard attempted to rationalize. "It will all be over soon, okay?"

"But it's never going to be over!" Hannah's voice was raised. "The agency will always come before me! It always has," her voice trailed off.

Harvard stood and took his daughter into his arms. "Honey, that is not true. You are my daughter - family. And I love you dearly. Nothing will ever change that." He kissed her forehead.

Hannah wiped the tears that had begun to stream down her cheeks. She disengaged herself from her father's embrace. "I don't remember ever spending a lot of time with you," she told him. Her words cut him to the heart.

"Where is all of this coming from, Hannah?"

"It's coming from *me*! Don't you understand how I feel?"

"Hannah, you know that I have to make a living." After he'd said the words he wished that he could retrieve them back.

Hannah threw her hands up into the air and gestured at their surroundings. "You've already made a living, daddy! Just look around you! We have more than what most people will ever have!"

Harvard remained silent.

"Daddy, you don't need to *make* a living anymore - you just need to *live* and enjoy what you've already made."

Harvard had never before heard his daughter speak so passionately about anything. For the moment he did not have a response.

Hannah continued, "You made me too, daddy," she stated emphatically, pointing to herself. "I didn't ask to be here - you and mom made me a part of your living. And now mom is not here anymore. Please don't keep ignoring me or brushing me aside as if I'm not here or as if I don't count. I am very much alive, daddy. And I *need* you to *live* with me."

Harvard felt defenseless.

"Hannah, I need for you to understand the situation here, and I need for you to be patient. We'll spend as much time together as you like when all of this is over."

Hannah shook her head in disbelief at her father's words. "That will never happen daddy and you know it!" she screamed at him. "Today its CorpAir - tomorrow it'll be another client. *You* have to be the one to decide when it's over, daddy."

He became frustrated. "Honey, I can't discuss this any further. Let's talk later this evening. I have an important meeting scheduled for this morning." Harvard kissed his daughter on the cheek and abruptly made his way into the house.

"Whatever you say, daddy. Whatever you say."

◈◈◈◈◈◈◈

The *Good Samaritan* was about to hang up after the cell phone rang three times with no answer.

"Hello."

"*Judas*?"

"Yeah, it's me."

"Can you talk now?"

"Not long," he whispered into the cell phone. "I got some people around the hangar."

"Fine. I just need for you to listen anyway," the *Good Samaritan* told him. "The device has been constructed. You need to be on the look out for a dark haired white male in his late twenties. He will be wearing a two-piece brown suit and carrying a thin, tan leather attaché case."

"Uh, huh."

"He will be visiting CorpAir's hangar next Friday sometime in the morning. All you have to do is give him access to CorpAir's new plane for at least five minutes without any interruptions. He will conceal the device aboard the aircraft at that time."

Judas thought for a moment. "But that plane ain't going nowhere for another week after the thing is planted," he uttered nervously.

"I'm aware of that."

"So then, I don't want that thing going off while I'm on the plane. I have to work on it still."

"The device is very sophisticated. It will be programmed to detonate on Friday July 25th at precisely 11:20 a.m. That's fifteen minutes after the flight has taken off."

"Okay. A brother can't be too careful."

"There's no need for you to worry," the *Good Samaritan* assured him.

"Hey, what about my money? I got some business to take care of."

"You know the agreement, *Judas*. One week from this Friday you'll get *fifty thousand dollars*. You'll get the other *fifty-thousand* once the job is completed."

"You mean once the sucker explodes in the air!"

"That's one way of putting it. Anyway, I have a meeting to get to. Remember, be on the look out next Friday."

"I hear you," *Judas* said before folding up his cell phone.

◈◈◈◈◈◈◈

When Harvard Prophet's secretary buzzed his telephone and announced that Dr. Hetzler was waiting to see him, Harvard quickly glanced at his watch. It was just shy of nine o'clock. Dr. Hetzler had never met with him at PPK's offices. Of course, Harvard had never told the doctor not to meet him here. Although, it was implied that for obvious reasons they were to meet at the doctor's office or some other less conspicuous place. He wondered what this impromptu visit was all about.

"Elizabeth, please show him in," he answered the secretary's call.

The door opened and as Dr. Hetzler entered the office, Harvard stood from his desk to greet him. He thanked his secretary as she closed the door behind her.

"Good morning, Phil," Harvard spoke reservedly.

Dr. Hetzler greeted him in return. Harvard escorted him to the burgundy leather sofa where they both sat down.

"Ordinarily, I would not have come here," Dr. Hetzler began to explain. "However, under the circumstances, I didn't see any harm."

"Meaning?"

"Well, as we speak, Duke Priest is meeting with his personal attorney to handle the transaction, so I knew that it would be safe for me to come to your offices."

"How can he handle the transaction without my presence?"

"Well, he indicated to me that he wanted his attorney to handle the matter. He wanted me to inform you that his attorney will forward the completed paperwork to the agency's law firm."

Harvard appeared skeptical.

"I suppose you have to understand how difficult of a decision this was for him," Dr. Hetzler added.

Harvard knew that he really didn't give a damn about how Duke felt about giving up his share of the agency. "So, what's next? Do we just sit and wait?"

"The shares are actually being transferred into your name as we speak. Duke understands that there will be no exchange of funds between the two of you until you've signed off on the deal as well. That's the paperwork he's having sent over to the agency's law firm. And, for your review, Duke said that his attorney will also fax over a copy of everything to you immediately."

Harvard nodded his head, still a bit skeptical.

"Therefore, Harvard, I was hoping that you and I could conclude our transaction."

"So, what you're saying Phil is that you want your money?"

"Well, our business arrangement is complete."

"Considering the fact that you show up here this morning unannounced, I don't happen to have $150,000 in cash sitting around anywhere," Harvard stated, a little perturbed by the doctor's audacity.

"Actually, you don't have to give me cash, I – "

"What! After you've insisted on nothing but cash payments all of this time!" Harvard interrupted him.

"What I mean is that I want you to have the funds wired directly into my account."

"Why?"

"I don't think that's really any of your concern. You owe me the money and this is how I want it paid to me."

Harvard resented the fact that someone else was attempting to order him to do something. He wanted very much to tell Phil Hetzler that he'd get his damn money when he gave it to him. But he did not want to jeopardize getting the fifteen-percent stake from Duke, so he acquiesced.

"Fine, Phil. Give me the name of your bank and your account number and I'll take care of the wire this afternoon."

"No, Harvard. We have to do this right now. I instructed Duke not to sign off on anything until he received my phone call this morning from your office. Now, I don't place that call until the funds are secured into my account. I have played by your rules, now I'm asking you to play by mine."

Harvard could feel his blood pressure began to boil. Who the hell did this little prick think that he was dealing with? Harvard stood from the sofa and walked over to his desk. "All right, Phil. Have it your way. I'll get my banker on the line."

Dr. Hetzler breathed a sigh of relief as he watched Harvard dial the number to his bank. He scribbled down the wiring instructions on a piece of paper and handed it to Harvard. Less than fifteen minutes later the money had been transferred. Dr. Hetzler waited another f ifteen minutes before calling his bank to verify that the funds had been received into his account.

After providing his banking representative with his mother's maiden name and verifying his social security number, his account balance was given to him over the phone. His new account balance was $150,025.00. It was correct. He'd withdrawn what little funds he had in the account yesterday except twenty-five dollars. The branch manager at his bank had already been instructed to transfer these newly deposited funds upon receipt, into an account he'd opened in Portland, Maine.

Dr. Hetzler was satisfied. The plan of retribution had worked. He wished that Duke had taken part of the money. In fact he'd offered it all to him. But Duke didn't want any of it. He said that he was satisfied just knowing that the money left the soiled hands of Harvard Prophet.

Dr. Hetzler prepared to leave. He told Harvard that he would call him later today to make sure that everything between he and Duke was in order. Of course, no such call would ever be made.

Harvard also felt a sense of relief to have finally gotten rid of one partner. Now, if all went well last night, he didn't expect to be seeing Princeton King around the office any time soon either.

CHAPTER TWENTY

"GOOD MORNING, THANK YOU FOR calling Prophet, Priest and King. How may I direct your call?" Adiva had only been answering the switchboard for about an hour and already she could tell that this was going to be a very busy Wednesday.

Adiva found it difficult trying to shake from her mind the close encounter she almost faced with Harvard last week. She realized now how foolish her actions had been. She could have gotten herself into some serious trouble.

There was no question in her mind now that Harvard Prophet was the mastermind behind the fatal mishaps that ultimately allowed PPK to remain agency of record for its three largest clients over the years. Adiva was equally convinced that Harvard was planning another mishap to try and thwart this current review with CorpAir. And she now had a possible date – *July twenty-fifth.*

She'd been reading the industry press lately. No one was predicting that PPK would hold on to its largest client. There were even rumors circulating that CorpAir had already decided upon its new ad agency – New York-based Young & Lucas.

Adiva realized that Harvard had to be aware of all this as well. The pressure was mounting for him to do something quickly. The final round of presentations were due in mid August. They were exactly one month away.

She was nervous about the fact that Harvard knew about her theory. It made it much more difficult for her to concentrate on her work. She was expecting him to summon her to his office at any given moment. And she faced another dilemma as well. Whether or not she should involve Hannah. She figured that Hannah could be useful in helping her to find out information, or even ultimately being the one to convince her father to call off this *D-Day* he was planning.

But the man was her father. Adiva didn't know if the girl would be willing to, in essence, bring her father down. And it was a catch twenty-two situation for Adiva. Once she broached the subject with Hannah, she wasn't sure of the possible repercussions. If Hannah refused to cooperate, undoubtedly she'd run straight to her father and the whole thing could get pretty ugly.

Adiva dialed Princeton's extension. They were cohorts in this thing and she needed to talk with him. But there was still no answer at his extension. She hadn't seen him at all this week. She really needed to alert Princeton to the fact that his office was bugged.

"Good morning, Prophet, Priest and King. How – "

"It's me, Adiva," Soupa Mann announced.

"Hey."

"Hey yourself. I just wanted to know if I could see you this evening?" he asked.

"I can't."

He sighed. "How long you gonna be mad at me?"

"It's not that, Soupa Mann. I have bible class tonight."

"Oh, yeah. I forgot today's Wednesday," he apologized. "Well, can we grab a bite to eat for lunch?"

"You know I only get an hour."

"Yeah, I know. That's why I was thinking fast food – ain't there a Burger King across the street from your building?"

"Not directly across the street, but there's one nearby."

"Hey, that'll work. You won't even have to lose your parking spot 'cause we can walk."

Adiva was reluctant. "That may not be a good idea," she told him.

"Aw, c'mon Adiva. Its just lunch!"

"I know. I just don't want to get into any more fights with you, Soupa Mann."

"Fights?"

"You know what I mean – arguments."

"Hey, I don't want none of that either. I just wanna see my girl and share some good news with her."

"What good news?"

"Can't tell you over the phone. You gotta meet me for lunch - noon at Burger King?"

She surrendered. "Okay. But I'll meet you there," she told him. There was no need for him to come up to the offices.

"Okay with me - be there or be square!"

"Bye Soupa Mann!" she giggled as she ended the call.

As she answered another incoming call, Adiva couldn't help wondering what his *good news* was all about.

◊◊◊◊◊◊◊

Harvard Prophet had just completed a call with CorpAir's CEO Douglas Sheldon. Douglas had been in Australia for the past week and he wanted to touch base with Harvard to see how things were proceeding. Harvard told him that they would be ready when the time came for final presentations. He also told him that he enjoyed his meeting yesterday with Christine Armstrong, and how he could see himself and his agency working together with her on many successful ad campaigns. Douglas thanked him for the kind words and wished him well during their presentation.

Harvard retrieved a dark green file folder from his attaché case. It was delivered to him late yesterday afternoon. The tab across the top of the folder read

Adiva Roberts' Background Check. He only had time to scan it last night.

He placed his *Ben Franklin* reading glasses on and began to peruse the one page computer printout. Harvard was surprised to discover that her boyfriend worked as a maintenance technician at CorpAir. He continued to read on. She lived with her eighty-three year-old grandmother. Her parents died when she was a toddler. She had no other siblings. She received a B.A. in Journalism, and she was a current student at The Portfolio Institute.

He had also double-checked on her requirement to complete a report on advertising as part of her graduation requirement. Everything appeared to be on the up and up. Then why was she poking her nose so deep into his agency? Harvard was particularly bothered by her interest in the mishaps. These events happened years ago. She had absolutely no business looking into matters that related to the agency's clients.

He realized that he could not allow her efforts to continue. Princeton didn't have sense enough to tell Miss Roberts to mind her own business when she brought the matter to him. So, he'd just have to take matters into his own hands. There would be no research report - at least not one involving Prophet, Priest and King.

There was a knock at his door.

"Come in," Harvard answered.

It was Seymour Boudreau. He approached Harvard's desk. "I'm terribly sorry to bother you, sir, but one of the men from the night cleaning crew brought this to me to give to you." He handed him a silver earring with a black pearl in the middle of it.

"What is this, Seymour?"

"One of the men from the cleaning crew apparently found it on the floor of your office last week when he came back to make a final check of the premises. He meant to give to you sooner. He said it was lying on the floor beside your desk." Seymour tried to shield the fact that he was a bit unnerved by the discovery. Who had Harvard been philandering around with in his office late at night?

Harvard examined the piece of jewelry. "I was up here late a couple of times last week. How late were the cleaning people here?"

"I don't know," Seymour answered dryly. "I believe that on the larger tenants in the building they always come back and make a final inspection just to make sure that their workers didn't omit anything. I would guess that it's probably after midnight at least when they would've come back around."

"Yes, I suppose so. I'm usually in my office until around eleven o'clock on ocassions. Of course, I can't say that I'm here to look for a piece of jewelry!"

"Of course not, sir."

"Well, it certainly doesn't belong to me. I am curious, however, as to how it got into my office."

"That I don't know, sir."

"Oh, well. Perhaps its rightful owner will surface." Harvard placed the earring inside his desk drawer. As Seymour turned to leave, Harvard called to him.

He turned around. "Yes, sir?"

"I just wanted to thank you again for that Aretha Franklin CD. It's really quite enjoyable."

"I'm glad you like it. Maybe we can listen to it together some time," Seymour responded, a broad smile crossing his face as he left the office.

◈◈◈◈◈◈◈

Harvard finished a call with one of the partners at PPK's law firm. He was informed that there had not been any contact from another lawyer with regards to the sale of Duke Priest's minority interest in the agency. Harvard became concerned. He also had not received the fax as Phil Hetzler had promised. It was almost noon, this should have occurred by now. Why hadn't he at least received a copy of the transaction papers from Duke's lawyer?

Harvard grew increasingly nervous as he skillfully wove his Jaguar through Atlanta's erratic late morning traffic. It wasn't so much the traffic that made him nervous. It was the fact that when he'd called Dr. Hetzler's office a short while ago, a recording came on that said the phone number had been disconnected. This sent Harvard scurrying from PPK's office tower. He was now driving north on Roswell Road to the office park where Dr. Hetzler maintained his practice.

When the elevator doors opened onto the fourth floor of the North Springs Office Building, Harvard stood patiently to one side as a young Asian woman and her toddler slowly exited. The young woman had the toddler strapped inside a stroller. She was encountering difficulty maneuvering the stroller from the elevator while trying to hold onto the child's diaper bag as well as her huge purse, which resembled a duffle bag.

Harvard kept his thumb pressed firmly against the *open door* button while the young woman continued her struggle to push the stroller through the doors. When she glanced over her shoulder at him, he feigned a smile, though his patience was wearing thin by the second. Finally, he reached over and took hold of the stroller and lifted it off the elevator for the young woman. He assumed she thanked him in some dialect because he could not understand a word she said to him.

When Harvard arrived at Dr. Hetzler's office suite, his nervousness turned into panic. Affixed to the door of the suite was a note on the doctor's letterhead stating that the practice had been closed permanently. He tried to enter the office but the door to the suite was locked.

"I'll be damned!" he shouted. Then he banged his fist against the door. His frustration could no longer be restrained.

As Harvard drove south on Roswell Road, back to PPK's offices, he was infuriated. He realized now that he'd been played for a fool. Apparently, Duke never had any intention of selling his stake to him. And Phil Hetzler knew it. Yet, he allowed him to pay out large sums of cash month after month.

The tables had been turned on him. It was a bitter pill to swallow.

Harvard realized that he couldn't confront Duke on the matter because then he'd have to explain his involvement altogether. The good doctor wasn't so stupid after all.

The Jaguar's entrance into the parking garage at PPK's office tower was less than smooth. "No one double crosses me and expects to get away with it," Harvard mumbled to himself as he slid the shiny black sedan into his reserved parking space.

Before he left Phil Hetzler's office building, he'd stopped at the building's leasing office to try and find out where Phil had gone. But the leasing agent told him, matter-of-factly, that she could not provide him with any information regarding their tenants - past or present.

Harvard remained unnerved. He'd eventually find the bastard. And when he did, he was going to annihilate him.

CHAPTER TWENTY-ONE

SOUPA MANN WAS ON HIS SECOND Whopper while Adiva had barely taken a bite of her fish sandwich at the Burger King, which was located just down the street from PPK's offices. The restaurant had become very crowded since their arrival forty-five minutes earlier.

Adiva was giving little attention to her lunch, which was spread across a brown plastic tray in front of her. As conversations from others within the restaurant erupted around them, she was focusing her thoughts, at the moment, on Princeton King.

Princeton had telephoned the office just before Adiva departed for lunch. He'd told her that he wouldn't be coming into the office today - again. She'd asked him if he was ill. And while he tried his best to assure her that he was fine, Adiva sensed from his voice that something was wrong.

After lunch she was going to make it a point to call him at home and try to get the situation clarified. Princeton had always been upbeat, as far she knew him. And if he wasn't ill, then something else had to be bothering him.

"Hey," Soupa Mann called out to her. "You better finish up that sandwich before I have to take it off your hands."

Adiva picked up her fish sandwich and handed it to him. "Here, you can have it. I don't have much of an appetite."

"Naw, baby. You eat it," Soupa Mann insisted. "I was only kidding."

She allowed the sandwich to drop down onto the tray. "Well, it'll just go in the trash."

Soupa Mann's face became twisted with concern. "You all right, Adiva?"

She gave him a reluctant sigh. "I can't really get into it now," she answered.

"Does it have to do with us?"

She shook her head. "No. There's a situation at work."

"What kind of situation?"

"I told you that I can't really get into it."

Soupa Mann displayed a look of mute appeal. "You don't trust me or something?"

Adiva reached for her soda and quickly took a sip. "It's not like that, Soupa Mann," she attempted to assure him.

"Then why can't you just tell me what the problem is, baby?"

She closed her eyes and began a slow, methodical massage of her temples. "Fine. But you have to promise to keep this between you and I, okay?"

Soupa Mann smiled broadly. "Who am I gonna tell?" he spouted rhetorically.

Adiva was about to dispel to him the basis for her lack of confidence in him when her cell phone began to ring. "Excuse me," she said, as she retrieved the tiny silver-colored flip phone from her purse.

Soupa Mann hunched his shoulders in a *don't-mind-me* manner and then he grabbed her fish sandwich and began to chomp away at it.

"Hello," Adiva answered.

"Hi Adiva, it's me - Princeton," his voice was dry.

"Where are you? Are you at the office?"

"No. I'm still at home." His voice was wooden and distant.

"What's wrong?"

"I can't explain right now. But, I called you on your cell phone because Lorraine said that you were still at lunch."

Adiva glanced at her watch. It was 1:05. She hadn't realized that her lunch hour had ended five minutes ago.

Princeton continued, "Listen, can you meet with me after work this evening?"

Adiva was hesitant. "Um, what time?"

"Around seven o'clock?"

She realized that meeting with him would mean skipping tonight's bible class. "This sounds important?"

"Very much so," he told her.

She would have to get Sister Williams to pick up Granny Rae and take her to bible class. "Um, sure. Where do you want to meet?"

"Well, do you mind coming to my house?"

She hesitated again. She knew that he lived farther north than where she lived. "You live in Alpharetta, right?"

"Yes. I can give you the directions."

She was familiar with how to get to the area, it was the traffic on Georgia Highway 400 that she was worried about. It could be horrendous during rush hour. "Okay, that'll work. Tell me how to get to your place." She pulled a piece of paper from her purse and began to scribble the directions on it. Soupa Mann's suspicious eyes were fixed squarely upon her.

"Who was that?" he asked demandingly after Adiva ended the call.

She told him that it was just her boss. Soupa Mann also wanted to know what the call was about. She wanted to tell him to mind his own business, but she didn't want it to appear that she was hiding anything. Reluctantly, she explained to him Princeton's request to meet with her after work.

"What you got to meet after work with your boss for?" Soupa Mann continued his inquisition.

"Well, I was about to explain things to you before I took the call," she answered him. "But I don't have time to get into it right now. I'm already late." Adiva took one last sip of her soda and then stood from the table.

Soupa Mann remained seated. "Oh, so it's like that!"

"Like what?" she responded, irritated.

"C'mon girl. You know what I'm talkin' about – don't play dumb with me!"

Adiva brushed herself off as she prepared to leave. "No I do not, Soupa Mann."

"I heard you ask what time to meet – so when after work are y'all gonna have this lil' meeting?"

"What difference does it make? I mean he's my boss – why you all concerned?"

Soupa Mann stood from the table, and as he did so he wadded up his napkin and threw it atop the tray amongst the other throw away items that had piled on it. "All I know is that, not more than an hour ago when I asked to see you this evening, you were quick to tell me that you had bible class – what's up with that?"

Adiva began to walk toward the exit. "Don't start trippin', okay."

"Naw, you the one trippin'," he corrected her, as he followed her out of the restaurant and into the scorching afternoon heat. "You don't have time to meet with me, but you all ready and willing to forget your bible class for your boss. I thought *Christians* were supposed to put God first, huh?"

"You don't even want to go there, Soupa Mann," she told him, accelerating her pace across Burger King's parking lot.

"Sorry baby, but I'm already there!"

"Well, don't expect me to join you."

Soupa Mann grabbed Adiva's arm and spun her around to face him. She jerked free from his grasp. "Don't be pulling on me, okay!"

"Listen to me, Adiva," he pleaded. "Why you acting like this?"

"Like what, Soupa Mann? You're the one copping the attitude!"

" 'Cause you acting like some crazy bi—" He interrupted the word and withdrew it before it shot from his mouth.

"Go ahead and say it, Soupa Mann," she prodded him. "I already know it's how you really feel."

He bowed his head and stared at the cement sidewalk beneath his feet. "Be that way," he mumbled.

Adiva didn't respond right away. She waited for traffic to clear before she darted across Peachtree Street. Soupa Mann scampered behind her. When they reached PPK's office tower, he asked her, "Can I walk you inside?"

"It's not even necessary," she answered. "I knew this would happen?"

"What?"

"Arguing."

Soupa Mann sighed heavily. "Well, I guess I just can't win anymore – at least not with you."

Adiva changed the subject. "What was your good news?"

"As if you really care."

"How can I care when I don't even know what it's about?"

They reached the main entrance to the building. "Well, it ain't no big deal . . . " he began. "It's just that . . . well, I'm finally gonna be able to get a professional demo tape made."

That was good news. Adiva knew how much Soupa Mann wanted to have a professional demo tape made of his singing. It was just one of the hurdles that he needed to overcome. The other one of course, was the money.

"Congratulations," she said sincerely. "When will the demo be made?"

Soupa Mann wasn't too good at modesty, though he attempted it. "Aw, it'll probably happen by the end of summer. I mean, I'll have everything in place by then."

"The last time you talked about making a demo you said that it was going to cost a lot to have it done professionally," Adiva said.

"Yeah, and it still is. I don't want something cheap. 'Cause if it's done cheap then I'm gonna sound cheap, and well, you know me – I ain't cheap."

"So, what'd you do – win the lottery?"

"Naw, just a lil' business deal that's coming through."

Adiva's eyebrows arched. "What kind of business deal?"

"A very profitable one."

"I hope you're not involving yourself in anything illegal."

"There you go – always got to think the worst." Soupa Mann's joy subsided. "Why can't you just be happy for me for a change?"

"I am happy for you. But I also don't want to see you get into any trouble."

Soupa Mann reached into his pocket and retrieved his pack of cigarettes. He held the pack of smokes in front of Adiva's face for emphasis, as he slowly pulled out a cigarette. She watched him in disbelief as he lighted the cigarette. He took a longer than usual drag. "News flash, baby," he whispered intentionally, as he puckered his lips and blew the smoke into Atlanta's humid air. "With you, I'm always in trouble." He took another drag of the cigarette before crushing it onto the sidewalk. "And ya know something else? I'm about sick and tired of your *holier-than-thou* façade. And, what really gets to me baby, is the fact that, if I'm such a poor lost soul in your eyes, then why you always beatin' me down rather than trying to lift a brother up, huh?"

Adiva remained silent.

Soupa Mann continued. "I ain't never told you I was perfect and I ain't never told you I was some Saint. But it seems like every chance you get, you got to find a way to remind me that I'm some low-life sinner. And then you want to turn around and invite me to go to church with ya – why? Tell me why Adiva Roberts? It ain't enough that you make me feel bad and ashamed, but you also want me to gather around a bunch of strangers so they can do the same too? Well, it ain't gonna happen!"

She made a feeble attempt to respond. "Soupa Ma . . . "

"Save it!" he interrupted her. "Just save it, 'cause I ain't trying to hear it. Ya see I'm the bad boy in your grand momma's eyes and apparently in your eyes too. And I'd be lying if I said none of it bothered me. But ya know what? Soupa Mann gon be all right – he gon survive just fine. So, you go meet with your boss this evening, Adiva. Forget that I ever asked for a moment of your self-righteous time. I might not be a bible scholar and all, but just remember this – sometimes you have to be willing to lend a heart in order to save a soul."

Atlanta's July summer heat couldn't keep Adiva's eyes dry. She surrendered to the band of tears that had bordered her eyelids. She couldn't have restrained the tears even with the help of Georgia's National Guard. She uttered no response to Soupa Mann's cutting words. He walked abruptly away from her, heading towards the parking garage. She could only watch him shrink away as he sidled his way through the crowd of people returning from their lunch.

CHAPTER TWENTY-TWO

HER EYES WERE SQUINTING AS SHE attempted to read the names on the fancy street signs that stood erect on every corner of Princeton King's country club subdivision. When she finally found the large brick mailbox that contained the address matching the one she'd scribbled on her notepaper, Adiva gazed at the huge house. It was no Prophet Palace, but it appeared just as stately and equally expensive by her economic standards.

She left the car parked on the street in front of his house as she made her way up the driveway toward the all brick home of Princeton King. As she neared the entrance, Princeton suddenly appeared in the doorway. "You could have parked in the drive," he told her, as he held open the front door.

"It's okay," Adiva replied.

The home was noticeably quiet as Princeton led her through the winding foyer and into the family room. "Where is everyone?" Adiva asked, looking around at the home's nice but simple furnishings.

Princeton did not answer her. "Can I get you something to drink?" he countered instead.

She politely declined, as she sat down on the overstuffed sofa. Princeton quickly turned on a couple of lamps, immediately brightening the room. He then took a seat in one of two matching overstuffed chairs that were positioned across from the sofa.

Adiva took notice of his scruffy appearance. He was dressed in baggy gray sweat pants with a black collarless cotton tee shirt. His face was starting to sprout stubble hairs. And his eyes appeared to be red as if he hadn't slept in days. She could sense that something was upsetting him.

"Glad you could make it," he uttered; failing to mask the pain he was feeling.

Adiva nodded and offered a slight smile.

"I know you want to know why I asked you to come here," his voice crackled.

She nodded again.

Princeton began staring at the floor and fidgeting with the platinum wedding band on his finger. It was obvious to the both of them that he was not only stalling, but quite nervous as well.

"Excuse me a moment," he said, as he leaped from his chair and rushed into the kitchen. "I need something to drink."

Adiva sat quietly as she listened to him open and close cabinets in his search for a glass. He called out from the kitchen and asked her again if he could bring her anything to drink. She declined for the second time. She found herself squirming a bit – unaware of what was forthcoming.

Princeton returned with a very tall glass of iced water. He consumed half the glass before setting it on a table that stood between the two chairs. He breathed a sigh of relief.

"Is something wrong, Princeton?" Adiva coaxed him. Her patience was diminishing rapidly.

Princeton allowed himself to make eye contact with her briefly before averting his attention to the floor again. This was not an easy thing to talk about. But he realized that he needed to share this with someone. And since he'd become not only close to Adiva since her hiring, but he also viewed her as a friend. He felt a sense of comfort around her.

"She finally did it," he said, barely audible.

"Excuse me?" Adiva responded, unable to decipher his words.

"She finally carried out her threat," he said again, in a more audible tone.

"Who carried out what threat?" Adiva remained confused.

"My wife - Muriel."

There was a moment of silence.

"I can't believe that she did it," he mumbled.

Adiva didn't want to push or pry. She assumed by now that maybe he just needed someone to listen.

"I shouldn't have bothered you, Adiva. I'm sorry," he apologized unconvincingly.

"It's not a bother," she tried to assure him.

Princeton consumed the remainder of the iced water, and then he began to open up to her. As he talked, he stared at the floor and sometimes at the mantle above the fireplace where a family portrait rested.

"Several years ago I had a slight drinking problem," he explained. Quickly interrupting himself, he then asserted, "Who am I kidding? I had a major drinking problem! And, at one point, it had gotten so bad that my wife threatened to divorce me and take the kids back to Illinois. It was a threat that I've lived with for quite some time."

Adiva was speechless. She didn't know how to respond.

Princeton continued, "Well, obviously I didn't want her to carry out her threat, so I pleaded for forgiveness . . . "

"Did she forgive you?"

"Yes. She forgave me and she made me promise to quit drinking alcohol. Well, I kept that promise for about six months before falling off the wagon."

"Did you go it alone or were you in rehab?"

"No, I never did the AA thing. I thought that I was capable of handling it on my own."

"It must have been tough. I can't imagine getting over an addiction like that without help," Adiva shared.

Princeton scratched his head. "I realize that now. But you know what? I was able to keep it a secret from Muriel for the past two years. I mean, I never came home drunk during that time."

"For two years?"

"Yep. I mostly drank a little at the office - you know, to get through a hectic day. But I made sure that I was sober before getting behind the wheel and driving home."

"So somehow, your wife found out about your continued drinking?"

Princeton stood from the chair and walked across the room. He stopped in front of the fireplace and retrieved the framed family portrait from the mantle and stared at it. "Yeah, somehow she found out," he whispered almost to himself.

Adiva felt sorry for her boss and friend. She realized that the loss of his family must have been tearing him apart inside. "Maybe she's just angry and hurt right now," Adiva offered. "Maybe she just needs a little time to cool off."

Princeton emitted a pessimistic chuckle as he placed the portrait back onto the mantle. "She's definitely gone for good."

"What makes you so sure?"

Princeton returned to the chair and sat down. "What you don't understand is that my wife has always wanted a way out of this marriage. Neither of us have been happy for quite some time. I gave her an opening and she decided to walk right through it."

Adiva was baffled by his candid revelations. "But what about the children? I mean she has to know the damaging effect that this will have on them."

Adiva didn't have children of her own, but she was all too familiar with the problems children of divorced parents sometimes faced.

"Muriel is only considering herself at the moment. I doubt seriously that she is contemplating the effects of separating the kids from their father."

Adiva nodded her head. "I am so sorry, Princeton."

He thanked her for her support.

"Do you have any idea how she found out that you were drinking again?"

"I've been racking my brain with that question over and over," he answered. "All I know is that when I got home last week, she and the kids were gone."

Adiva's eyes widened. "You mean she didn't even confront you?"

Princeton shook his head. "No. According to her letter she had all the proof that she needed." He walked over and retrieved the letter that was still lying on the floor beside the fireplace. He handed it to Adiva. "Here, read it for yourself."

Adiva just stared at it, unsure if she should be reading something so personal. "It's okay - read it," Princeton told her.

Reluctantly, she read the one page letter. It tugged at her heart. She also realized that she was in no position to judge Muriel King. She had no idea of what it must have been like for Muriel to live with someone who had a problem with alcohol. And, although Princeton was nothing less than the consummate gentleman around her, she knew that there were always two sides to every story.

"I'm really sorry that you have to go through this right now," Adiva said, referring to the stress he must also be facing with the CorpAir review looming.

"Well, this couldn't have come at a worst time that's for sure," Princeton acknowledged.

As silence enveloped the room momentarily, Adiva stared at the letter again. Suddenly, one of the lines written by Muriel stood out before her – *I know all about your drinking at the office* . . . AT THE OFFICE!

"Oh my god!" Adiva shouted.

"What?"

Adiva handed the letter back to Princeton and covered her face with both of her hands. Tears streamed down her face. "I know how she found out," she sobbed.

"Adiva, what are you talking about?" Princeton asked, as he sat beside her on the sofa, his arm resting around her shoulder.

"It was the package," she continued sobbing.

"Package?"

Princeton finally got Adiva to calm down. She reluctantly shared with him her little invasion into Harvard Prophet's office last week and her subsequent discovery of his secret room where he made recordings of the entire office. She told him that she was certain that Harvard Prophet had taped him drinking in his office and that he must have had a reason for wanting his wife to find out, so he had the tape sent to her.

Princeton was skeptical. "Harvard is an eccentric man, Adiva, but even this would be a bit much."

"I know it may be hard to believe, but I'm pretty sure that's how your wife found out."

Princeton was still unconvinced. "Not possible."

"Princeton, it is possible. I know because I sent the package," she admitted.

"You what?"

Adiva explained to him how Harvard had brought her a brown envelope, which she now realizes contained a VHS tape, and had requested that she address it to Muriel King and to have it sent by courier to his home.

Princeton's face grew flush with anger. "That conniving son-of-a . . . " he stopped himself and quickly exhaled. "So he's been privy to everything I've done and said within the privacy of my own office!" He stood from the sofa and kicked over the coffee table. His action startled Adiva, causing her to jump. "Damn him! He did this just to try and get rid of me somehow. Maybe he thought that I'd be so preoccupied with trying to save my family that I wouldn't have time for the agency and then he could easily strike!"

"What do you mean, strike?"

"Harvard has always wanted Duke and I to sell our remaining thirty-percent to him. Apparently, he's willing to go to great lengths to get his hands on it." Princeton walked over to a wall in the family room, coiled his fist and punched it through the sheet rock. "I'm going to kill that old goat!" he yelled.

"Princeton, please calm down, okay."

"Adiva, that man has to pay for what he's done!"

"I know. But killing him won't bring your family back. We've got to be rational. Harvard Prophet is about to be brought down – real hard."

He gave her a bewildered glance. She decided to bring him up-to-date on her theory. She shared with him that she was even more convinced that Harvard was behind the mishaps involving the agency's reviews. And she told him that she was convinced that he was planning a major mishap of some kind to try and thwart the current CorpAir review. Princeton now believed that Harvard was capable of anything.

"Princeton, I need for you to continue on as if you're not affected by what Harvard has done to you. I mean I need time to pull everything together. If you go and confront him, it could stifle everything, okay?"

Princeton hesitated. "If what you've told me is true, then why hasn't he caused something to happen already to thwart this review?"

"Trust me, he's planning something. And I got a feeling that it's going to be sooner rather than later."

Princeton face displayed concern. "Adiva, you just might be in over your head, don't you think?"

"Maybe. But I can't turn back now. Innocent people have lost their lives over the years because of this man's obsession with maintaining a certain client roster. He must be stopped!"

"As unbelievable as it all sounds, it appears to be within the realm of Harvard to engage in such actions." Princeton shook his head in disbelief. "Well, let me know what it is you need for me to do. I certainly don't have much of anything else to lose at this point."

Adiva breathed a sigh of relief. She explained to him that she wanted him to continue on with everything being business-as-usual. They agreed not to have any more meetings within PPK's offices on this matter. She jotted down his cell and pager numbers. She also apologized to him for not being of much help in the situation with his family. He told her not to worry. He was going to get his kids back eventually. But for right now, he wanted to make certain that Harvard Prophet paid dearly for the havoc that he'd wreaked.

CHAPTER TWENTY-THREE

PRINCETON KING CONDUCTED HIS Thursday morning creative session in a business-as-usual manner, as discussed with Adiva. Duke Priest had joined the group during their final hour of presentations and brainstorming. Conspicuously absent, however, was Harvard Prophet.

Now that he was fully aware that his office, as well as others, was bugged and monitored via hidden video cameras, Princeton was overly cautious when he spoke. And he'd gotten rid of the beer that was maintained within his office.

He still hadn't been able to reach his wife in Chicago. He was certain that she was staying with her parents. Of course, her parents did have Caller ID, so he figured that they were screening his calls. He decided not to sweat it. If he never saw Muriel again he would function quite nicely. His two children were the ones who mattered most to him. He was their father and they loved him and he loved them.

Princeton was now sitting at his desk replaying in his mind his discussion with Adiva yesterday evening. She was proving herself to be a very perceptive and intelligent young woman. He was amazed how she'd gained impeccable insight into

Harvard during her less than two-month tenure on the job. He'd worked with the old man for ten years and had yet to figure out his eccentric antics.

Princeton dwelled for a moment on the agency's past account reviews. How could Harvard be so cold-hearted and ruthless? If in fact he was responsible for those client mishaps. Was keeping an account on the agency's roster that important to him? Fighting assiduously to hold onto an account was one thing, but killing for it was quite another.

As unbelievable as it all seemed, Princeton was compelled to give validity to Adiva's theoretical conclusions. It appeared true that Harvard Prophet had determined in his mind that if he created a mishap or some major chaos surrounding their client during the midst of an account review, that perhaps he could persuade the client to delay, postpone or call off the review altogether. And sadly, his demented thinking was correct. Prophet, Priest and King had never lost a client during its ten years as an ad agency – now Princeton King knew why.

He and Adiva had both agreed that Harvard couldn't have pulled all of this off by himself. Someone else had to be working with him. Perhaps several others. But, at the moment, they could not determine whom the accomplice or accomplices were. Nor could they act on what they believed until they had concrete evidence. It was paramount that all of their ducks be in a row before they even considered approaching the authorities.

Adiva had told him that Harvard had circled Friday, July 25th as the *D-Day*. Was he actually planning to destroy a CorpAir plane with some kind of an explosion? And if so, how could he and Adiva determine which flight he was targeting? CorpAir maintained a fleet of over one hundred aircraft. They would need solid proof just to warn CorpAir or the FAA of the possibility that one of their planes were being targeted for an explosion. And he realized that they simply could not afford to open that door until they were fully prepared for the ensuing consequences.

Surprisingly to him, Adiva had mentioned that she could try and get Hannah Prophet to assist in gathering more information. He'd laughed at her notion. How could she even consider asking the man's daughter to help them bring him down – effectively destroy her own father? But Adiva was somehow convinced that it was at least worth trying. She reasoned that with Hannah living under the same roof as her father, she would be in an ideal position to listen for any kind of clues, look over his notes, and even get her father to confide in her about his plan. Of course, it all seemed a long shot to Princeton. Nevertheless, it was a shot they had to pursue.

The panoramic view from his seventeenth floor corner suite made everything below appear insignificant. The momentary respite that he was afforded from an afternoon that consisted of a steady stream of conference calls from once loyal PPK clients provided Harvard Prophet with a much-needed solace.

As he stood, peering through the windows within his office, he attempted to sort out the myriad of issues that were confronting him. The fact that Duke Priest had duped him into thinking that he would relinquish his fifteen-percent stake in the agency, and the fact that, although he'd given Princeton King's wife the ammunition she needed and sought to leave her good-for-nothing husband, the man was behaving as if all was right in the world. Harvard began to feel that his efforts were seemingly for naught. He'd also failed at arranging an afternoon luncheon yesterday with CorpAir's CEO Douglas Sheldon. He resented the very notion that Douglas had been avoiding him. Since the review was announced, they hadn't played one round of golf together. He thought their paths would at least cross at the Golf Club of the South. No such luck.

Harvard was now convinced that CorpAir had no sincere intentions of selecting PPK to remain as their agency-of-record. His scorn for the way many clients dragged agencies through this meaningless review process intensified with each passing year. The bastards more often than not already knew which agency they wanted to align themselves with well in advance of their announcing a review and shamefully inviting a select few to pitch for their prized possessions. He could never quite understand the logic in spending countless numbers of hours as well as money on what would undoubtedly amount to a vain attempt to hold onto a client – a business relationship – that had long since suffered from disintegration. If wrenches hadn't been thrown into PPK's past reviews, then the agency would have never achieved the level of success and acclaim that it has today.

Harvard turned from the window and allowed his tiring eyes to survey the immaculate surroundings of his spacious suite. A lot of ideas had been created in this very room, he pondered. This was where he'd made some tough decisions. It was a somber reflection. The loss of CorpAir would place everything he'd worked so hard for in jeopardy. Their seventeenth floor haven would be nearly impossible to maintain if their annual billings were cut in half. The majority of the PPK staff would have to be let go. Others would probably follow CorpAir to their new home, while the rest would simply defect to agencies that were once regarded as the enemy. *Advertising with the enemy* – there was a bit of irony to the thought.

Harvard's personal stature within the community would also be weakened with the loss of the $50 million account. And no matter how much of a positive spin would be put on the loss, he, as well as others, would ultimately see himself as having failed. He shuddered at the very thought.

It was utterly arcane that the success or failure of Prophet, Priest and King – his agency, should be resting in the hands of one client. It simply wasn't fair. It wasn't prudent. And Harvard now realized, more than ever, that it would be up to him to make absolutely certain that it wasn't going to happen.

◈◈◈◈◈◈◈

The *Good Samaritan* met with the young white, handsomely dressed man in the front seat of his car. They were discussing tomorrow afternoon's meeting at CorpAir.

"How will I know him?" the young man asked.

"You won't. He has a description of you and what you'll be wearing. When you enter the hangar, he'll approach you."

The young man nodded.

"He will also ask if you've been sent by the *Good Samaritan*. And, of course you will nod in the affirmative. He will then lead you to the designated aircraft."

The young man continued to listen carefully.

"He will grant you access for five minutes. That is all the time you'll have to conceal the device in the library which is located near the rear of the plane."

"That's plenty of time," the young man uttered confidently.

"As you are leaving, be certain to take clear notice of the gentleman you've just met. You will give him this envelope . . . " The *Good Samaritan* handed the young man a fat, brown envelope stuffed with fifty-thousand dollars in cash.

The young man grinned wickedly as he felt the weight of the envelope in his hand. "It's too bad this gentleman won't get the opportunity to spend one dollar of this cold, hard cash, isn't it?"

"Indeed, it is a shame. But it's just as well. The poor fool would have only wasted it."

The young man reiterated his instructions. "So, after I give him the envelope and take a good look at him, I will wait in the parking lot for him to leave work, which should be around four o'clock. Then I will follow him home and finish him off, right?"

"Yes. But make certain that you retrieve the envelope."

"Definitely. My wages are in there."

"Only half of it goes to you, understood?"

The young man grinned wickedly again. "Yeah, right. I give the other twenty-five back to you for safekeeping."

The *Good Samaritan* ignored his sarcasm. "Just make sure the operation is a smooth one."

"Don't worry. It's the only way that I know how to operate," the young man remarked. "Hey," he whispered, as if others were listening. "You know that *Sade* singer? Well, when she sings *Smooth Operator*, she's singing about yours truly!"

"Whatever."

CHAPTER TWENTY-FOUR

THE DIGITAL CLOCK THAT WAS BUILT into the switchboard seemed to be moving slower than ever. Adiva was anxiously awaiting her three o'clock break. Twenty more minutes had to tick away first. She didn't have time to eat lunch this afternoon so her stomach was growling louder than an angry lion. The several cups of coffee she drank didn't help either. She'd gone to the restroom more times within the last two hours than she had on any given day before.

Finally, the clock displayed the magical time she'd been waiting for. And right on schedule, she could see Lorraine heading her way to relieve her. It was about time girlfriend showed up on time for her break.

"Girl, you don't know how long I've been waiting to see you," Adiva told Lorraine as she walked up to the receptionist counter. "I've had to pee for the last forty-five minutes!"

Lorraine looked as if she could care less. "Listen, Adiva. Go ahead and go the restroom, but when you get back, you will need to go and see Seymour Boudreau in his office."

Adiva wondered what he wanted to see her about. "Sure. Why am I meeting with him?"

Lorraine shook her head. "I don't know. He asked if he could meet with you as soon as possible. But don't worry, the phones will be covered."

Adiva told Lorraine that she would meet him just as soon as she returned from the restroom.

Seymour Boudreau was PPK's thirty-something vice president of media. She remembered Lorraine telling her about him during her initial interview. She'd said that he was black in terms of skin tone, but he was born and raised in Paris. Adiva rarely saw him around the office nor had she any direct interaction with him, other than transferring calls to his office.

When she arrived at his office, his door was opened slightly. She knocked softly. With his sleeves rolled back, he was rapidly clicking away on his computer keyboard that sat atop a credenza behind his desk. He didn't hear her knock. She waited before getting his attention. She couldn't help but notice how large his office was. He wasn't even a partner, yet his office was much bigger than Princeton's.

"Mr. Boudreau," she finally called to him.

He quickly turned around. "Hello, Miss Roberts. I'm sorry that I didn't hear you arrive." He stood from his plush leather chair and extended his hand to shake hers. "Please, have a seat. And allow me to first thank you for the excellent job you've been doing on the switchboard. I've heard nothing but positive feedback from around the office," he said in his thick French accent.

Adiva forced a smile. She could feel a knot beginning to form inside of her stomach. Why did Mr. Boudreau want to meet with her? Maybe she'd screwed up one of his calls?

"Before I get to why I wanted to meet with you, Miss Roberts, I must ask something of you?"

"Sure - okay," Adiva answered nervously. She stared vacuously at his dark, clean-shaven complexion as a lecherous smile slowly formed across his face.

"Miss Roberts, I was simply wondering if perhaps you might know to whom *this* belong?" he asked, as he produced, with a happy flourish, a black and silver pearl earring.

She recognized it immediately. She'd searched all over in her car and at home for the missing earring last week. "Yes, it belongs to me, Mr. Boudreau," she answered. "I realized that I had lost it last week, and I'd almost given up on ever finding it again."

There was a slight hesitation from Seymour. "Well, it seems that my instincts were correct. You see, when Mr. Prophet found this and brought it to my attention, you were the first person who came to mind. I mean, you dress quite fashionably and - well, it appeared to be something that suited your taste."

Adiva blushed at the compliment. "Thank you. Where was it found?"

He seemed to stammer for a reply. "Uh, it was found in the mailroom - lying next to the postage meter. It must have fallen off while you were stamping the mail."

Adiva realized that he'd just lied to her. Lorraine had never shown her how to prepare the mail and she'd never even been in the mailroom. The only mail that she'd handled was the *package* that Mr. Prophet had given her last week to send to Princeton's wife, and that was sent by courier.

Then she remembered. The last time she'd worn the earrings was last Wednesday, and it was after she'd gotten home later that night that she discovered one of the earrings was missing. She realized now that it must have fallen off while she was crawling around in Harvard Prophet's office. Her heart began to accelerate. So, he knew that she'd been in his office. And now he was sending Seymour Boudreau to try and gauge her reaction. She had to play it cool.

"Of course," she replied. "Well, I'm glad that it was found." She took the earring and placed it inside her purse.

Seymour gave her a critical squint as he observed her reaction. She wasn't going to let him see her sweat. "Well, now. I suppose we've solved the case of the missing pearl," he attempted to humor her. "Shall we now discuss the real reason why I wanted to meet with you," he said matter-of-factly.

Adiva simply nodded.

"Miss Roberts, I wanted to discuss your school project or paper that you've been working on."

She quickly exhaled. "Whew! I thought that I was being fired," she uttered, relieved.

"Fired? Good gracious, no! Whatever gave you that idea?"

"Well, this meeting I guess," she answered, feeling somewhat foolish, yet regarding him cautiously.

"Relax, okay. This is not a termination meeting. In fact, I've never had to fire anyone before in my life. I am, however, concerned about this paper."

"Concerned? What do you mean?"

He hesitated. "Let's say we cut to the chase. Miss Roberts, I'm very sorry to have to tell you this, but apparently the management team met on this matter and it has been decided that we do not want you interviewing anyone else about this agency, nor do we want you conducting any further research into the agency's activities and/or clients."

It was a curve ball that flew right past her. She was speechless. "I . . . I don't understand?"

"Listen. I'm sure you can appreciate the fact that the agency is currently experiencing a very arduous time. I know your paper may seem like a harmless little project, but this agency is a privately-held organization and we simply do not wish to make public certain information."

"Mr. Boudreau, I'm practically done with the paper. Besides, I wouldn't have time to start all over on another subject," she tried to plead her case.

"Again, I'm very sorry, Miss Roberts. But the decision has been made."

She was flabbergasted.

Seymour decided to answer a call while he allowed her to digest the bitter pill.

Harvard Prophet had to be on to her. Now he was apparently trying to stop her efforts to find out the truth behind his so-called success.

Seymour must have gotten a call from France because he began to speak in French. As she sat waiting for him to finish the call, she watched him roll down the sleeves of his shirt. The cuff of his left sleeve caught her attention. His initials were embroidered on the cuff in gold letters - *S.B.* Suddenly, she realized where she'd seen the initials before - it was on the bath towel in Mr. Prophet's bathroom! Seymour Boudreau and Harvard Prophet were sharing a bathroom? Unbelievable! It was now obvious to her who Mr. Prophet's accomplice was - Seymour Boudreau. Lorraine had told her that rumors were circulating that Mr. Boudreau was gay, but she never would have figured that Harvard Prophet was.

It was all starting to make sense. Harvard Prophet was the mastermind behind the mishaps and Seymour Boudreau carried out the dirty details. Just as he was doing now, trying to shut her up.

Seymour completed his phone call. "So, Miss Roberts, do we understand one another on this matter?"

Adiva wanted to tell him off. Let him know that she was on to the both of them. But she knew that she needed to remain cool, calm and collected. "Sure. I understand," she pacified him. Of course, she had no intentions of backing away. Her mind had already been made up. Harvard Prophet was a dangerous man. The clients on PPK's roster were no more than pawns to him. He seemed to have made a game of the whole advertising agency business. And in his own eccentric way, he'd convinced himself that he was doing something noble. Now it was up to her to try and put an end to his deadly game - even if it meant endangering her own life as well.

CHAPTER TWENTY-FIVE

ADIVA ROBERTS MET WITH PRINCETON King early Friday morning at a Starbucks that was located one block from PPK's offices. It had been agreed upon that they would no longer hold meetings or discussions together within the office. They were getting very close to putting all of the puzzle pieces together and they couldn't afford any snags or delays.

It was a humid July morning. Adiva glanced at her watch as she waited for Princeton to return to the small corner table with their coffee. She had one hour until she had to be at the switchboard. They needed to make the most of their time this morning.

"Here you are," Princeton said, handing the cup of coffee to Adiva. He sat in the chair across from her. "Why do we drink this hot stuff when it's ninety-degrees outside?" he asked rhetorically.

"You said that you had some additional information?" Adiva asked, not wanting to waste any time on small talk.

"Yes. I do," he answered, and then he quickly fished a small note pad from the inside breast pocket of his red blazer. "I know why Harvard may have circled Friday, July 25th on his calendar," he began. He took a sip of his coffee before continuing. "That is the day that CorpAir will have its inaugural flight to San Francisco. It didn't dawn on me until I was reviewing my own calendar yesterday."

Adiva found this revelation very interesting. "What's the significance of this flight?" she asked him.

"Well, for one thing, it is expected to be filled with some of Atlanta's most prominent figure heads, including CorpAir's CEO himself."

"That would be significant."

"The flight is number twenty-nine hundred and it is scheduled to depart Atlanta at 11:05 in the morning for non-stop service to San Francisco. This is expected to be a lucrative market for CorpAir."

Adiva shook her head. "If Mr. Prophet is planning to create a mishap from one of CorpAir's flights, this would definitely be the one to use."

Princeton agreed. "Blowing up that flight would be a major catastrophe for CorpAir," he remarked. "But there's absolutely no way we can let that happen, Adiva."

"I'm with you. My parents were killed in a plane crash," she spoke solemnly.

"I didn't know that," he said. "I'm sorry."

Adiva cleared a tear from her eye. "So, I would not want anyone else to suffer that kind of a loss."

"We're going to need more concrete evidence. I mean we can't go running to the authorities with what we think Harvard is planning to do. The man is very well connected in this city," Princeton stated.

"How do we get concrete evidence?"

Princeton scratched his head. "I'm not sure. But, if you can convince his daughter to try and help us, then it might strengthen our chances."

"I'm already moving in that direction," Adiva told him. "I'm meeting with Hannah later this evening after work."

"Tread softly, Adiva," he advised. "I mean, until you're certain that she's on our side, don't reveal too much information to her – we don't want her running back to daddy."

"Yes, I'm aware of that possibility."

Princeton and Adiva discussed whether or not they should involve Duke Priest. "I believe that it's still too soon. Let's wait until we have more evidence. It would be much easier for Duke to carry on with business-as-usual if he didn't know what the old man was up to," Princeton explained.

"I guess you're right." Adiva then shared with Princeton her meeting yesterday with Seymour Boudreau. She included her belief that not only is Seymour the other person working with Harvard, but that the two of them might be involved in an intimate relationship.

"Well, it would certainly explain Seymour's obsession with pleasing the old man," commented Princeton. "Imagine that – Harvard Prophet a gay man . . . no wonder he never remarried or involved himself with another woman after his wife's death."

"The man does seem to have an interesting life," remarked Adiva.

Princeton had a thought - "You know, Adiva - if push comes to shove, Seymour might be the one for us to put the squeeze on."

"How?"

"Well, if we can get him to talk - spill his guts - on the premise that he could save his own hide, he could very well be the link we need to bring down the old man."

Adiva wasn't so sure. "I don't know. Lorraine seems to think that Seymour Boudreau is very loyal to Mr. Prophet."

"Maybe so. But there comes a point in time when every man's loyalty is put to the test. If he knows the fan is about to hit the fire, perhaps he'll start thinking about saving himself."

"I guess we can reserve that card and play it if it becomes necessary," she responded.

"It can't hurt."

She drained her remaining coffee from the cup and prepared to leave for the office. "It's time for me to head to the office," she told Princeton, strapping her purse over her shoulder.

"Of course." Princeton stood from the table and gave her a hug. "You're an incredible young woman, Miss Roberts," he whispered in her ear.

Adiva smiled, embarrassed a little.

"All right, then," she said, breaking the awkward silence. "I guess I'll see you at the office."

As she departed first from the Starbucks, Princeton stood and watched her - his eyes ranging freely up and down her diminutive figure.

CHAPTER TWENTY-SIX

THE HANDSOME, YOUNG WHITE MAN SAT nearly crouched in the driver's seat of a dark brown late model sedan. He was wearing dark glasses over his eyes as he surveyed the employee parking lot at CorpAir's headquarters near the airport.

It was now Friday afternoon. Everything had gone as planned earlier that morning. The explosive device was tucked away beneath a seat in the library of the CorpAir jet. It was set to detonate fifteen minutes into the flight - 11:20 a.m. on Friday, July 25th - one week away.

He'd also gotten a good look at the African-American gentleman who, for the moment, was fifty thousand dollars richer.

The young man peeked at his watch. Four o'clock on the dot. He began to observe carefully as workers began streaming from CorpAir's hangar. A new shift would be coming in. The workers all appeared to be blue-collar types - maintenance technicians mostly. They joked and laughed with one another as each one headed to their respective automobiles - some made their way to the MARTA rail station across the street to wait for the train home. He imagined that the first thing they'd all probably do when they got home would be to rid themselves of the denim overalls that clung to their bodies. It had to be at least ninety-five degrees outside. He appreciated the coolness of his car's air conditioner even more as he watched their sweat-drenched bodies scrawling across the parking lot.

He grew nervous as the parking lot emptied. There was no sign of the African-American gentleman. He waited awhile longer. After an hour had passed, he picked up his cellular phone and punched in some numbers.

The *Good Samaritan* answered on the third ring.

"He never came out of the building," the young man spoke.

"What do you mean?"

"It's after five now and there's been no sign of him."

The *Good Samaritan* became angry. "How could you just let him get away?" he barked.

"Hey, my eyes have been fixed on this parking lot all afternoon! The guy never came out of the building!"

"Are you saying he's working late?"

"I don't know – maybe."

"Hold on a minute!" The *Good Samaritan* placed the young man on hold. He pushed the button on his telephone console to get another line and quickly dialed *Judas'* number at CorpAir. There was no answer. He immediately dialed *Judas'* cell phone.

"Where are you *Judas*!" he shouted when the cell phone was answered.

Judas recognized the *Good Samaritan's* voice. "My main man!" he greeted cheerfully. "I'm just cruising down the interstate heading home - what's up boss man?"

"Why aren't you at work?"

"Well, first of all, it's after five o'clock and . . . "

The *Good Samaritan* quickly interrupted him. "I'm talking about before now! I called you at work earlier this afternoon and you were not there," he lied.

"Oh, yeah right. Well, you see, after my lil' business meeting was finished this morning I decided to leave early. You know, take care of a lil' shopping errands."

The fool was already spending the money. "*Judas*, something important has come up and I need to meet with you as soon as possible."

"Uh, okay. But it's gon cost ya!"

"What?"

Judas erupted into laughter. "Just kiddin' boss man! My pockets are pretty phat right now!"

Not for long, The *Good Samaritan* mused to himself. "I need for you to be home at nine o'clock tonight, all right?"

Judas thought for a moment. "Yeah, that's cool."

"I'll be sending the young man who you met with earlier today. He'll give you all the details of what's going on."

"No problem."

"Good. I'll need your address and directions to your apartment."

Judas rattled off his address and directions. "Hey, boss man. Is there a change in plans?"

"Don't worry about it – just a little snag that we need to take care of and we need your help. I'll make sure that you're rewarded for your troubles."

Judas grinned fiercely. "Now that's what I like to hear! *Rewarded for my troubles* – sounds like music to my ears!"

When the *Good Samaritan* returned to his call with the young man, he quickly outlined the new plan. "Listen, he's already started spending the money, so it probably won't be exactly fifty-thousand," he told the young man.

"What!"

"Don't fret over it. You'll get yours."

The young man relaxed.

"Just make certain that you get every cent he has left. You also need to take his cell phone – we'll need to destroy it. And while you're there, search the place for anything else that might be incriminating and get rid of it, understood?"

"You got it."

"Good. Call me as soon as it's all over. And let's not have anything go wrong this time."

The young man resented the insinuation. "Hey, it wasn't my fault the dude left work early!"

"Just live up to your name - *Mr. Smooth Operator.*" The Good Samaritan clicked off the phone and resumed his attention to matters pertaining to the agency's clients. He couldn't wait for all of this to be over. It was driving him absolutely insane.

CHAPTER TWENTY-SEVEN

WHEN ADIVA ARRIVED AT THE BUCKHEAD Fish Market on Friday evening, Hannah Prophet was already waiting for her at the bar. She was sitting quietly. Her tall, thin body straddled the swivel barstool. For the past ten minutes she'd been daydreaming as her hand robotically fed bite-sized pretzels into her mouth. Adiva recognized her immediately by her dangling blonde French-braided ponytail.

"What's up, girl?" Adiva spoke as she joined Hannah at the bar.

"Hi."

"Been waiting long?"

"No. Actually I just got here a few minutes ago."

"What are you drinking?" Adiva asked.

"A daiquiri."

"It better be virgin!" Adiva admonished her, like the typical older sister.

"It is – just like me!" Hannah remarked, hoisting her glass into the air.

The two girls burst into laughter.

"So, I haven't seen you around the office much this week – you playing hooky girlfriend?"

Hannah chuckled. "Of course not. I was helping Seymour Boudreau with a special project," she explained.

"Oh. What do you think of him?"

"Seymour?"

"Yeah."

"Well, I'm not around him that much. But I'll say that he's a pretty intense guy."

The bartender asked Adiva if he could get her something to drink. "Sure, a Diet Coke will be fine," she told him. "I hear he's pretty loyal to your father."

"Who isn't loyal to my father?" she posed the question rhetorically.

"Do I detect some animosity?"

Hannah sipped more of her daiquiri. "Daddy and I kind of had a fight the other day," she confessed.

"Really? About what?" Adiva continued to try and get her to be at ease.

"Well, we hardly spend any time together. I mean I know he's real busy with the agency and all. Especially trying to save CorpAir. But I really thought that we'd get to spend some quality time together this summer."

Adiva hesitated before responding. "I'm sure he would love to spend time with you if he didn't have so much on his plate right now."

"That's just the thing, Adiva. Daddy's plate is always full with something. Today is CorpAir – tomorrow it'll be another client. I told him I was sick of it all. I mean I know he wants me to take over the agency someday, but I really don't want any part of that corporate squirrel run."

"You mean *rat race*."

"Well, they both involve running. Anyway, advertising is not what I want to do with the rest of my life."

Adiva realized that she had to broach the subject. "Hannah, I need to have a serious conversation with you."

"About what?"

"Your father."

"Daddy? Oh dahling, the fight was no big deal, we fight all the time - he'll get over it."

"No, not about your fight with him."

"Then what is it about my father that you need to talk about?"

"First I ask that you hear me out, okay?"

"Sure."

"Hannah, how much do you know about PPK?"

"In terms of what?"

"I mean do you know much about the agency's operations, clients, etc.?"

"I know a little."

"Are you aware that the agency has never lost a client since starting ten years ago?"

"I'm aware of that."

"Well, doesn't that strike you as a bit odd?"

"No. Why should it? I mean daddy's very good at what he does. And he's very competitive. I'm sure you know that it's a doggy doggy world out there."

"What?" This one even threw Adiva for a loop.

"You know, cut throat."

"Girl, it's *dog eat dog* world!"

"Fine. You keep up with these things, I don't."

Adiva let out a deep sigh. "Hannah, I know he's good at what he does. But how many agencies go ten consecutive years without ever losing a client? And more than that, how coincidental is it for account reviews to be postponed due to catastrophic events every time there's a review announced?"

Hannah looked confused. "What are you talking about?"

"You realize that the agency is fighting hard to keep CorpAir as a client, don't you?"

"Yes. And daddy's very confident that the account will stay with the agency."

"Do you know when was the last time CorpAir placed their account up for review with PPK?"

Hannah thought for a moment. "Not exactly. Probably when I was still in high school."

"It was five years ago," Adiva told her.

"I was a senior then."

"Anyway, the review got all the way to final presentations before CorpAir had to postpone it, which eventually led them to calling off the review altogether."

"What does all of this mean and what does it have to do with my father?"

"What I'm trying to say Hannah is that I don't believe that the CorpAir review that was cancelled five years ago was a coincidence."

"Well, I don't know why it was cancelled."

"I do. It was cancelled because CorpAir's marketing chief at that time was murdered."

Hannah stared at Adiva saucer-eyed. "What! How do you know all of this? Daddy never said anything to me about anyone from CorpAir being murdered!"

"Well, that's exactly what happened."

Hannah sipped more of her daiquiri. "What are you trying to say, Adiva?"

Adiva wanted to choose her words carefully. "I really don't know how to say this . . . "

"My god, just say what you have to say! Stop walking around the shrubs!"

She means *beating around the bush.*

Adiva exhaled long and hard. "Hannah, as you know I've been doing a lot of research on PPK for my school paper. And, well . . . what I've discovered is that your father may be the one responsible for the murdered CorpAir executive."

Hannah clasped her hand over her mouth, obviously shocked at the revelation. "How dare you accuse my father of such a thing?"

"Believe me, Hannah. I'm not trying to hurt you or anything like that. But, from what I've gathered, it appears that your father not only caused the Corpair review to be halted, but he's also done similar things for three other accounts, and each of them involved some catastrophic event." She went on to explain the other client mishaps.

"You're lying, Adiva!"

"I wouldn't lie about something so serious. Trust me. I know that this must be very hard for you to accept and even understand."

"I don't want to hear anymore," she told Adiva, unable to restrain her tears.

Adiva placed her arm around her. "I'm sorry, Hannah. But we need your help."

"*We*?"

Adiva explained to her that Princeton King was aware of her beliefs and that he fully supported her.

Hannah let out a hysterical laugh. "Princeton? That drunk belly! He's always been jealous of my father. I wouldn't believe him if he was the last person on earth!"

"He's a smart man, Hannah," Adiva defended her friend and boss.

Hannah sneered at her remark.

"I have a strong belief that your father is going to do something big-time to stop this current review from happening?"

"Like what?" she asked reluctantly.

"Well, it appears that he may be planning an explosion aboard one of CorpAir's flights."

"That's ludicrous! He wouldn't do anything like that! Have you completely lost your mind, Adiva?"

Adiva remained silent.

"If you and Princeton have everything all figured out, then what do you need from me? I mean, why haven't you gone to the police with your *beliefs*?"

"We don't want to rush into anything without solid evidence. Our objective isn't to put your father behind bars, Hannah. We want to prevent him from blowing up a plane and destroying innocent lives!"

Hannah looked away from her.

Adiva continued. "What we need from you is help in trying to figure out exactly how your father is planning this attack."

"Wait a minute," Hannah asserted. "Are you asking me to spy on my own father?"

"I wouldn't call it that. But we've got to find out his plans before it's too late."

"No, Adiva - *you've* got to find out! I don't want to be part of this craziness of yours. And, I will not stand by and allow you to falsely accuse my father of these heinous acts! I can't believe you - my father hired you! He gave you a job. Is this your way of thanking him?"

"Hannah, I'm very grateful to be working at PPK. But I can't just close my eyes and look the other way. And neither should you!"

"Well, I think that you've made all of this up! I bet you're just trying to embellish your school paper so that you'll receive a good grade!"

"No, that's not it, Hannah. This is very serious. Let me ask you this – did you know that your father has a secret room in his office?"

Hannah hesitated. "Obviously not, if it's *secret*," she replied sarcastically.

"Well, he does. And inside it he has all of these television monitors. He tapes what everyone else is saying and doing. Hannah, all of the offices are bugged!"

"Big deal, Adiva! He owns the agency. He has to keep up with what's going on."

Adiva had the urge to slap the naïve girl. "Keeping up is one thing, invading someone's privacy is another!"

"You've only been working at the agency since last month, what makes you such an expert on my father or PPK?"

"It doesn't matter. What matters is that your father is so obsessed with not allowing PPK to lose a client from its roster that he's going to extreme measures to keep it from happening."

Hannah shook her head in disbelief. "I still don't believe you. I know my father, Adiva. He's not capable of murder!"

"Hannah, anyone is capable of murder given the right set of circumstances."

"Well, daddy isn't! And I'm tired of listening to your horrible lies! I'm going to tell my father about your wild accusations and I know he's going to fire you on the spot!"

Adiva grew nervous. "Listen to me, Hannah," her voice was pleading. "If that's what you feel you have to do, then fine! But, understand this - what if I'm right? Huh? Let's just suppose that I'm right about your father. What happens then?"

"You're not right about my father!"

"But what if I am?"

Hannah didn't respond. She took the paper napkin that she was holding and dabbed her eyes. She didn't want her tears ruining her make-up. "I have to leave now," she told Adiva.

Adiva watched as Hannah paid for her drink and then hurriedly exit from the restaurant, her ponytail swinging swiftly from left to right.

As she drove home, she thought about what had just occurred. She realized that they needed Hannah in their corner. Her reaction was exactly what she would have expected, but hoped wouldn't happen. After all, Harvard Prophet was her father. And they were asking her to turn against him. To help bring him down.

She thought about what Hannah had threatened to do. If she did tell her father and he fired her, she decided that it wouldn't keep her from continuing forward. Harvard Prophet needed to be stopped. He was no longer running an advertising agency. He was playing a very deadly game.

CHAPTER TWENTY-EIGHT

THE HARD KNOCK ON THE DOOR SOUNDED around 9:05 p.m. *Judas* had been eating a bowl of popcorn and watching television. He was somewhat tired from all the shopping he'd done earlier, spending a little more than three thousand dollars on new clothes, a new watch, and three pairs of shoes.

Right on time, he thought to himself as he strolled over to open the door. The young white man that he'd met earlier today at CorpAir stood on the other side of the door. The dark brown suit was gone. He was dressed in jeans, a collar-less white silk shirt and a black blazer.

"So, we meet again," *Judas* greeted him.

The young man immediately shuffled his way past Judas and inside the apartment. "Close the door and lock it," he instructed *Judas,* looking wildly about the room.

Judas resented his tone and apparent attitude, but he complied.

"You alone?" he asked, still studying the apartment.

Judas nodded. "Yeah, why?"

The young man became irritated. "Listen, I ask the questions, got it?"

"Hold up!" *Judas* shot back. "You ain't gon come up here in my place and try to tell . . . "

At that precise moment the young man quickly pulled a revolver from inside his blazer and pointed it directly in front of *Judas'* face. "And tell you what?"

Judas took a step back, remaining silent as he shifted his focus between the revolver and the young man.

"Over there! Up against the wall!" he ordered, pointing to the dining room area.

Judas began to back away slowly. "Hey man, we're on the same team here," he said cautiously.

"Just keep quiet!"

When Judas reached the wall in the dining room area he was then ordered to face the wall and to place his hands behind his head. His mind was racing. What was going on here?

"Where's the money?" the young man demanded.

Judas played dumb. "What money?"

It was a bad decision. The young man became even more irritated. He walked over and shoved *Judas'* face into the wall with full force. *Judas* doubled over in agony. Then he felt the young man's elbow smash into his back, sending him to the floor recoiling in pain. "Don't play games with me, *bro*!" the young man gritted, as he took a couple of steps backward, still aiming the gun squarely at *Judas'* head. "Now, I will ask you again – where's the cash!"

Judas' body was still convulsing with pain. He could feel a sickening wave of terror welling up from within the pit of his stomach. He tried to make sense of what was happening. Apparently, the *Good Samaritan* had set him up. "It's . . . it's not here," he managed to utter. "But I can go get it," he added quickly, hoping to ward off any additional body blows.

"You're not going anywhere!" the young man snarled, as he walked over to *Judas'* writhing body to deliver a swift kick. But just as he brought his leg forward, *Judas* somehow mustered up the strength to grab hold of the young man's foot, sending him tumbling backward. The revolver flew from his hand and slid across the hardwood floor and came to rest beneath the sofa.

Oblivious to the pain in his swollen face and his aching back, *Judas* was on top of the young man instantly. Their two bodies became intertwined as they rolled back and forth, knocking over the dining room chairs. *Judas* was much stronger than the young man, despite the pain piercing through his body.

The young man attempted to roll *Judas'* body off his, but to no avail. *Judas* then balled his right hand into a tight fist and pounded it into the young man's face, catching him squarely in the left eye. The young man's voice exploded from the excruciating pain. But before he could even absorb the full impact, another blow pounded him again. He then felt *Judas'* hands wrap around his neck. His voice degenerated into a childish whimper as he gasped for air.

"He set me up, didn't he?" *Judas* yelled at the young man, though he already knew the answer. The young man was unable to respond as *Judas* increased the pressure, squeezing his neck with gripping force, as he watched the young man's handsome face become etched with desperate terror.

Just before the young man was about to pass out from a lack of oxygen, *Judas* released his grip. The young man gasped violently for air. *Judas* ran over, lifted one end of the sofa and retrieved the revolver. The gun was equipped with a silencer, so he knew that he could finish the young man off without attracting attention.

"Get your butt up!" he yelled.

The young man slowly got to his knees, and then struggled to his feet. He was sucking in air as quickly as he could, as blood slid down his face. *Judas* pointed the revolver at him. "Give me your car keys," he ordered him. The young man fished the keys from the front pocket of his pants without hesitation and slowly handed them to *Judas*. "Now, I'm gonna give you exactly one minute to get out of my apartment and out of this neighborhood before I start firing," he spoke deliberately.

The young man bolted from Judas' apartment like a kicked dog. *Judas* watched from his living room window as the young man dashed down the apartment building's steps and then sprinted across the parking lot, never even giving a second thought to the dark brown sedan he was forced to leave behind.

Judas took a moment to compose himself. He touched the area of his face that just minutes ago had made uneventful contact with the wall. He flinched from the pain. Realizing that it wasn't safe to remain in his apartment, he quickly retrieved a suitcase from the hall closet and began filling it with the new clothes he'd purchased earlier. After he had all that he felt he'd need for the next few days, he thrust his hand between his bed mattress and pulled out the envelope containing roughly forty-seven thousand dollars in cash. It was doubtful that he'd ever see the balance of fifty thousand dollars due him, so he knew he needed to make sure that this money was spent wisely.

He didn't bother straightening up the apartment before he left. Time was of the essence. He didn't know if the young man would return with an entourage to try and finish him off. He should have finished the guy off, but killing just wasn't in the cards for him, even though it would have been self-defense.

He loaded the suitcase into the back of his vehicle. As he sped from the parking lot, he grabbed his cell phone and punched in some numbers. It was time for the *Good Samaritan* to do some serious confessing.

◊◊◊◊◊◊◊

Adiva had waited until Granny Rae was sound asleep before she phoned Princeton. When he answered his phone she told him all about her unproductive meeting with Hannah. He was deeply disappointed to learn that she had been unsuccessful in trying to get Hannah to join them in their efforts. Now, he was even more worried about what Hannah would do next.

"I say we prepare for the worst case scenario," Adiva said.

"That being?"

"Well, that she's going to spill her guts to her father."

Princeton gave an exasperated sigh. "It was a risk I suppose we had to take."

They decided that they'd get together over the weekend and discuss a game plan to combat Harvard's reaction should his daughter choose to divulge what she knows. They realized that time was running out. If no other solid evidence developed soon, they would simply have to go to CorpAir or the authorities with what they believed. The bottom line - CorpAir flight 2900 had to be grounded next Friday - whatever the cost, whatever the consequences.

CHAPTER TWENTY-NINE

JUST BEFORE MIDNIGHT, *JUDAS* ENTERED his room on the twentieth floor of the posh hotel just outside of Atlanta. He'd hide out here until he could get a handle on what was going on. He'd been unable to reach the man who apparently held the answers.

His back still ached and his face remained swollen. He flopped down in a winged-back chair next to the bed. He pulled his cell phone from his pocket and dialed the *Good Samaritan's* number again. Finally, he answered.

"I guess you ain't expect to be hearing from me, now did ya?" *Judas'* voice was tight, edged with tension.

There was a moment of silence on the other end of the phone.

"What's the matter, *Good* Samaritan? Cat got your tongue? Or, should I say the devil?"

The *Good Samaritan* tried to think quickly. He'd never heard a word from the young man. The idiot must have fumbled the job again. "*Judas*! Am I glad to hear your voice," he lied unashamedly. "Are you all right?"

"Save it, boss man!" *Judas* retorted. "I know you tried to have your lil' flunky knock me off tonight."

He tried to sound mortified. "What! I did no such thing!" he sniffed with haughty denial.

"You can cut the act!" *Judas* told him. "'Cause as you can hear, I'm alive and kicking. And unless I get some straight answers, I'm gon be kicking your bald-headed a—"

"Let's not rush to judgment," the *Good Samaritan* interrupted, his face growing flush.

Judas chuckled to himself. "Funny you should use that word - *judgment.* Because your game is over, boss man. It's judgment day! Now, I want you to listen and listen good . . . "

The *Good Samaritan's* hand was wet from perspiration as he gripped the phone. He swallowed hard, but remained silent.

Judas continued. "You came to me with this lil' proposition. I heard what you had to say and I eventually agreed to what you offered. Now, all I had to do was allow your lil' flunky five minutes on the plane - which you said would be plenty of time for him to plant some kind of explosive device. Well, I did my job, and I know that he did his."

The *Good Samaritan* sat on the edge of his bed and listened nervously.

"Now, for some reason you decide to try and double-cross me by having this punk kill me in my own apartment and take my money – money that I earned!"

"Judas, you don't understand . . . "

"Oh I understand all right!" *Judas* yelled into the phone. "Now, I don't know why you want to blow up that plane, and it really don't concern me. 'Cause I ain't never killed anyone before and I ain't trying to start. Otherwise, I would have put a couple of caps into your lil' flunky tonight."

The *Good Samaritan* breathed a little easier. The guy wasn't into killing.

"But I just might be willing to allow you to be the first person I decide to waste," *Judas* added.

The *Good Samaritan* felt a sudden stab of anxiety in his gut. "There's been a big mistake," he offered, trying to control his quavering voice. "Things just got out of hand. I'll make it up to you, *Judas*."

"All I want from you is the rest of my money."

"Of course. You'll get your money. As promised. But the deal was that you'd get it after the twenty-fifth, remember?"

"Huh! That deal died when you tried to have me whacked," *Judas* told him.

"Stop accusing me of that!" he shouted, amidst his frayed nerves.

"What – you can't stand the guilt?" *Judas* chided him. "Well, here's the new deal," he began as he went on to explain that he wanted the remaining fifty thousand dollars wired into his bank account no later than Thursday morning - one day before the twenty-fifth - or he was going to find him and finish him off.

Reluctantly, the *Good Samaritan* agreed. At least for now.

"Good. And I don't want any more surprises," *Judas* remarked.

When their conversation ended, the *Good Samaritan* threw his cell phone across the room. It smashed into the dresser before scattering into pieces onto the carpeted floor. He felt a horrendous headache forming. The pressure was getting to him. He walked into the bathroom, opened the medicine cabinet and quickly popped two pills into his mouth. He took a small *Dixie* cup that sat on the sink's countertop and filled it with water and then he washed the pills down.

"I really need a good night's sleep," he mumbled to himself as he climbed back into the bed. He knew that he just needed to get through this next week and then the pressure would be off.

CHAPTER THIRTY

ADIVA TRIED WITH VERY LITTLE SUCCESS to shield her nervousness while she operated the switchboard on Thursday morning. It was approaching mid morning and she hadn't seen or heard from Hannah all week long. It became crystal clear to her that Hannah would spill her guts to her father. Adiva was convinced that it was only a matter of time before she was summoned into Mr. Prophet's office and handed her walking papers. But until that calamitous moment arrived, she realized that she still had a job to perform.

As the switchboard continued to supply her with one call after another, she gave it her best effort at answering each call with a smile, which she hoped her voice inflected. Her fingers, with their neatly polished nails, moved swiftly across the numbered rows of buttons as she transferred calls to their appropriate destination. At times she felt like a traffic cop. And it was up to her to keep things moving steadily along. She was careful not to leave any caller on hold for any extended period of time, for that could quickly create a traffic jam. And for those calls that came back to her unanswered, she would re-route them to voice mailboxes or jotted down messages with sheer precision. Perhaps if she continued to remain this busy she wouldn't have time to think about being fired.

Princeton King stopped by Adiva's desk and motioned for her to meet him in five minutes downstairs. When the time came, she got Lorraine to cover the phones.

The two of them stood outside the entrance to the first floor cafeteria. "Any word from Hannah?" Princeton was eager to know.

Adiva shook her head. "Not a word. Nor have I heard anything from Mr. Prophet."

"Well, that could be a good sign," Princeton said. "Because if she'd spoken to Harvard, you or I, or both of us, would certainly know it by now."

Adiva agreed. "Maybe my talk had an effect on her after all."

"Let's hope so. In the mean time, I say we still play things cool," Princeton advised. "And, I don't recommend that you try and call Hannah."

"I hadn't planned on making contact with her," Adiva replied.

"Good."

They then decided that it was time to bring Duke Priest up to speed. He was a partner in the agency, and right now they could use another ally. Princeton said that he would try and get a meeting scheduled with Duke sometime later that day. He would inform Adiva of the time and place.

"Hey," she called to him, as he headed toward the elevator to go back upstairs first.

Princeton turned around.

"Any word from your wife?"

"Nope," he answered.

She cast him a despairing look. "I'm sorry," she said to him.

"No need to be," he replied and then disappeared into the elevator.

◈◈◈◈◈◈◈

Harvard Prophet knew the importance of appearing in absolute control. The agency was less than a month away from giving the presentation of all of their lives. PPK's key staff members were assembled in a small conference room that was adjacent to Harvard's executive suite. He stood tall before them at the head of the oval-shaped mahogany wood table.

If there was a smell to power, there was no mistaking the scent of power that emanated from Harvard Prophet's towering presence in the room. The custom-made, black pearl, *Hugo Boss* suit that draped his body was befitting a man whose no-nonsense approach to the advertising agency business was being emulated by comrades and adversaries alike throughout the industry.

Although this was not a scheduled meeting that he was about to preside over, it was a meeting that he deemed vitally important. Essential to all of their survival. Rumors were being propagated throughout the press that a mass exodus of PPK's staff was about to take place. Harvard would not tolerate defections by anyone. PPK had always hired the best and the brightest. The agency paid its people well, eliminating their need or desire to lurk in the shadows of other agencies, trying to see if the grass was in fact greener on the other side. And, when headhunters came knocking, PPK's employees were not shy in the least in telling them to go elsewhere.

Harvard remained standing as he surveyed the room. Two chairs at the table, one on his right and the other on his left, were conspicuously vacant. Princeton had chosen not to sit on Harvard's right, where he usually sat during meetings, and Duke had decided to skip the meeting altogether. Princeton had lately sensed some tension between Harvard and Duke.

Harvard motioned with his hand for Seymour Boudreau to move to the seat on his right. Seymour quickly obliged him. He then had his vice president of human resources move to the seat on his left. Now, everything was in order.

He made it a point to say good morning to each of the key staffers present prior to taking his seat at the head of the table.

"PPK has always been a survivor," he began. "And I underscore the word *survivor*." He thanked them and he praised them for their enormous efforts poured out over the past weeks on behalf of the CorpAir review. He reminded them that while they were near the finish line, the race wasn't quite over. He wanted, however, to tell them to prepare to celebrate because victory would be bestowed upon them as it had always been in the past. But even his level of confidence in retaining their $50 million jewel had been tarnished.

"I know that some of you are concerned about the future of this agency should we lose CorpAir. But I am here to tell you that whether we're chosen to remain agency-of-record for CorpAir or not, PPK will not succumb to a *has-been* advertising agency!" His rhetoric continued for an additional half-hour. And he hoped that they were buying into his every resounding word.

Harvard paused from speaking. All eyes were squarely upon him. It then occurred to him just how much they were depending upon him to pull them through this crisis.

"Listen to me," he continued. "PPK has already made its mark. Our reputation has been tempted and it has been tried throughout our ten years of existence. We've been the envy and the scorn of our industry counterparts. But as you all can very well see, Prophet, Priest and King is still standing!" He took a sip from the glass of water that had been placed in front of him. "The very core of our foundation has been shaken! And I am not so naïve as to think that this crisis hasn't caused some of you to begin planning your next move elsewhere. However, such actions would greatly displease me. But, I do understand your fear." He reached for his glass and sipped more water.

"My fellow comrades, I appear before you this morning to say to you that PPK will ride out this boisterous storm! We will win this hard fought battle! We will overcome this seemingly insurmountable obstacle! My friends, WE WILL NOT FALL!" The old man's eyes welled up with tears as he banged his fist against the conference table. A cold chill ran down the spine of each of them. Seymour wanted to reach out and hug him. Even Princeton was moved by the emphatic speech. Then someone at the other end of the table began a slow clapping of his hands. As each clap became more rapid, others joined him in the room until all of them stood in a rousing applause around the conference table. Harvard remained seated. His heart was beating prodigiously. It filled him with great elation to know that he had their full support.

This could very well be your last stand, Princeton thought to himself. Harvard Prophet's day of reckoning was fast approaching.

CHAPTER THIRTY-ONE

ADIVA ROBERTS STARED CATATONICALLY at the switchboard after terminating the last call. Late Thursday afternoon she'd phoned Soupa Mann at CorpAir and was told that he hadn't shown up for work all week. His supervisor mentioned that he hadn't seen or heard from him since he left work early last Friday.

Adiva's face was stricken with fear. She'd also tried all weekend to reach him at home, but he didn't answer the phone. And when she'd tried his cell phone it just rang.

Throughout the afternoon her face grew haggard with worry. After she'd shut down the switchboard for the day, she remained at the receptionist desk. She didn't know what to do. Finally, she surrendered to the tears that she'd been fighting back all afternoon. Something terrible had happened to Soupa Mann – she could feel it. She put her head down on her desk and sobbed.

"You can stop worrying," Hannah said to her as she stopped by the receptionist counter.

Adiva looked up and was surprised to see Hannah standing before her. "I didn't say anything to my father," she told Adiva. "Not yet anyway."

Adiva began to dry her eyes with the back of her hand. "Why didn't you?" she was curious.

"Well, it's not because I believe a word of what you said," she was quick to point out. "I just want to be fair. "I'll give you and Princeton until tomorrow to prove what you've been saying," she told Adiva.

"Actually, that's about all the time we have anyway," Adiva said solemnly. "Friday is the day something is going to happen."

"Well, I hope you two are wrong. But, I'll try and help anyway that I can. But I will not do anything to harm my father, Adiva. You know that blood will cling closer no matter how much water you pour on it."

She means *blood is thicker than water.* Adiva decided to allow the miss-stated cliché to pass. "You're doing the right thing, Hannah," Adiva thanked her.

"Well, I'm not so sure. Anyway, quit your crying before I get started."

Adiva dried her eyes some more. "I was crying for a totally different reason," she confessed.

Hannah turned on her southern charm. "What's the matter, dahling?"

Adiva thought about Soupa Mann again. "I think something horrible has happened to my boyfriend," she said.

"What?"

"We had lunch together last Wednesday, and . . . well, it turned into an argument, so I decided to back off from him and let things cool for awhile. I mean it wasn't as if I didn't have enough on my mind already. But, when I tried to call him over the weekend, there was no answer at his apartment."

"Oh, Adiva dahling – maybe he just went away for the weekend or something. You know how men are."

"No. I don't think so. You see I called him at work this afternoon too. His supervisor told me that he hadn't shown up for work all week long," Adiva explained, unable to restrain more tears from flowing.

Hannah walked behind the receptionist's counter and placed her arms around Adiva. "I'm sure he's all right," she tried to console her.

Lorraine Brown had just left her work cubicle to leave for the day. As she passed through the front area, she noticed the two women embracing. "Hi guys! Everything okay?" she asked them.

Hannah explained why Adiva was upset. Lorraine offered her some encouraging words as well. "Thanks," Adiva said to Lorraine. "But I'm just going to drive over to his apartment after I leave here. I won't feel better until I know that he's all right," she told them.

"Do you want me to come with you, dahling?" Hannah offered.

"Thanks, Hannah. But I'll be fine. I will call you later tonight, okay?"

All three women engaged in a group hug before they left PPK's offices.

◈◈◈◈◈◈◈

Princeton King stopped by Duke Priest's office again for the third time today. It was empty. He couldn't imagine where the guy was. It didn't surprise him that he chose not to attend Harvard's little pep rally this morning, but he didn't expect the guy to stay away from the office all day. He felt a little guilty about not involving Duke in this matter about Harvard once he figured it out with Adiva. But, he realized that the guy had been fighting hard lately battling depression. Princeton wished that he could have done more to help. But it wasn't as if he didn't have his own personal problems to contend with. Life was just plain difficult right now for a lot of people.

◈◈◈◈◈◈◈

The *Good Samaritan* was pleased with himself. He didn't think that he could pull it off, but he was able to convince the manager at *Judas'* apartment building to unlock the door for him. At first the middle-aged woman adamantly refused – citing residents' privacy policies. But once he flashed the five, crisp one hundred dollar bills in front of her face, she couldn't unlock the door fast enough.

Once inside, he locked the door behind him. He removed his horn-rimmed glasses and began to wipe them with a white handkerchief retrieved from his hip pocket. When the spectacles appeared to be clean, he put them on again and began scouring the apartment. He ransacked drawers, over-turned tables and even smashed a few things. He wanted it to look as if someone was looking for drugs or money. That way, when he took care of *Judas* for good, the police might think that a drug deal had gone sour or maybe someone had botched a robbery attempt. He'd also decided to leave some cash behind for good measure.

As the *Good Samaritan* continued to rummage around the apartment, he made an abrupt halt in his actions. His eyes became fixed on an eight-by-ten framed photograph of *Judas* and PPK's new receptionist. They were snuggled tightly within each other's arms. The photo appeared to have been taken in a park somewhere. He walked over and lifted the photograph from atop the large screen television.

"Well, well. What do we have here," he whispered, a traitorous smile forming across his bearded face. He had no idea that there was such a close connection between *Judas* and their very own Adiva Roberts! What a small world.

"*Judas,* my boy – you think you're in the driver's seat, do you? Well, I say you get ready for a new driver!" The *Good Samaritan* began to laugh triumphantly.

Amidst his laughter, he heard a key being inserted into the lock of the front door. Who could that be? For a moment he panicked. Unable to move. But just before the door was opened, he darted into the kitchen and wedged himself behind the doors of the small laundry room.

Adiva emitted a shrill scream after stepping into the apartment. The place looked as if a tornado had blown through. "Soupa Mann!" she called out, running to the far end of the apartment to check his bedroom. She clasped her hand over her mouth when she saw that his mattress had been over-turned, clothes were strewn about and broken items lay everywhere. She didn't know what to think.

A startled gasp escaped from her mouth when her cell phone began ringing inside of her purse. Her hands shook wildly as she pulled the phone from her purse and answered it. "Hello," her voice was strained.

"Adiva, it's me – Soupa Mann."

A sudden burst of adrenaline raced through her veins. "Where are you!" she shouted, her voice raising an octave.

"Calm down, baby," he told her. "I had to get away. I'm just outside Atlanta."

"Why? What's going on?"

"Listen, I'll explain everything. But first I need to know something . . . "

"Know what?"

"Remember that time, right after you got your new job, when you were telling me that your ad place worked on my job's account?"

"Yes. CorpAir."

"Right. And do you remember telling me how y'all was getting ready for some kind of *interview* 'cause CorpAir wanted new ad people?"

"Yes. It's called an agency review."

"Well, how did that ever turn out? I mean did y'all get to keep the account?"

"No – I mean, the final stage of the review isn't until next month, why?"

Soupa Mann smacked his forehead. "Now it all makes sense!"

"What? What do you know about the review?"

"I don't know nothing 'bout the review. But I do know who's trying to stop it from happening," he told Adiva.

"Who?" she shouted in eager anticipation. She could hear the pulse of her heartbeat roaring in her ears.

"Well, I think it's the owner of your agency."

"I knew it!" she screamed. "I knew it was him!"

"Baby, that's not the half of it," Soupa Mann began to explain. "You see, the man came to my job last month. I don't why he picked me – I guess 'cause I had access to the planes," he answered his own question. "He offered me, get this – " Soupa Mann paused for effect. " – the guy offers me one-hundred thousand dollars just to let someone on one of CorpAir's planes!"

"Why?"

"Well, I would find out later that the guy must have a beef with CorpAir about something because he wanted to plant a bomb on one of the planes."

"Oh my god, no! Tell me you didn't do it, Soupa Mann?"

There was silence on the other end.

"You did it, didn't you?"

"Listen, baby. I didn't think about it at the time. I mean we're talking about one-hundred G's!"

"Do you realize that this man is planning to kill a bunch of innocent people? These people lives are worth more than money!"

"I know that now. That's why I'm trying to fix things," he told her.

"Is the bomb planted on flight 2900?" Adiva asked him.

He thought for a moment. "Well, I'm not sure of the flight number, it's the plane that CorpAir pulled aside to get ready for some special flight to San Francisco tomorrow morning."

"That's it! Soupa Mann we've got to do something!"

"I know, baby. I feel real bad about all this. I mean, all I was thinking about was the money and how it could help me get my demo made and all . . . "

"So that's the *business transaction* you were talking about last week?" she interrupted him.

"Well, yeah I guess."

"I just can't believe this," she said.

"Well, I should have known that the guy was up to no good. I mean can you believe that after he gave me half the money, he hired someone to try and kill me to take the money back!"

"Are you serious?"

"Yeah! This lil' white dude showed up at my apartment last Friday night with a gun to shut me up for good. But I fought him off though."

"So this is why your apartment is such a mess?"

"What? Adiva, tell me you're not in my apartment!"

"Yes. It was the only place I knew to come to start looking for you."

"Baby, you got to get out of there! It's not safe! That bald-headed dude could have somebody staking out the place!"

"What bald-headed dude?"

"The owner of your agency, who else! He calls himself the *Good Samaritan*! He's good all right - good for nothing! He's the one who set all this stuff up!"

"Wait, slow down Soupa Mann" she told him. "First of all, the owner of PPK is not bald. Gray but not bald."

"Naw, this dude is bald on top and he's kinda short and stocky - with a facial beard. And, oh yeah, he wears them *John Lennon* glasses!"

Adiva didn't realize that her cell phone had just dropped from her hands and fell to the floor. She was reeling with astonishment. Soupa Mann had just described *Duke Priest*! He was the mastermind behind all of this? Her head began to throb. This is unbelievable! Hannah was right all along. Harvard Prophet was innocent.

"Hello, hello!" Soupa Mann's voice piped through the cell phone as it lay on the floor. "Adiva! You still there?"

As she was about to bend down and pick up the cell phone, the arms quickly wrapped around her small body from behind. She immediately let out a hysterical cry. Soupa Mann heard it and became frantic. "Adiva! Adiva!" he yelled into his end of the phone.

"Shut up and you won't be harmed!" the familiar voice told her. He then cupped his hand over her mouth. She struggled to free herself from his grasp, but she wasn't strong enough. He dragged her into the kitchen and pinned her down on the floor until he had securely tied her hands behind her back with an extension cord. Then he found some masking tape in one of the kitchen drawers and he strapped some across her mouth. He then stood her up.

Adiva was horrified as she stared into the face of Duke Priest.

"Hello, Miss Roberts," he grinned wickedly. "It seems as if we have something in common – or shall I say, *some one*." Duke grabbed hold of her arm and led her back into the bedroom. He retrieved the phone from the floor.

"Good evening, *Judas*!" he spoke in a wicked tone of voice.

"What you doing in my apartment! What you done to Adiva!" he shouted, his nostrils flaring.

"Absolutely nothing. At least for the time being," he sneered.

"Don't you touch her! You hear me!"

"Now, now *Judas*. This is not the time to make idle threats. You do as I say and all will be just fine."

"Yeah, right! Like I'm supposed to trust you after what you tried to do to me!"

"Still holding a grudge, I see. Well, quite frankly, *Judas*. I don't believe that you have much of a choice."

"Man what you want!"

"You know what I want, *Judas*. And when I get it, we'll then discuss what you want," he emitted a sinister laugh.

"What you mean, *discuss*?"

"I don't mince words, *Judas*. The explosion will take place as scheduled, you understand? And until that time, I advise you to sit tight and try not to get in my way, because if you do, then I'll have no alternative but to take my anger out on this nice young lady." Duke ran the back of his fingers across Adiva's cheek. "She has such a pretty face, doesn't she?"

"I'm warning you, you sicko!"

"*Judas,* it's not nice to call people names. Besides, you didn't think I was a *sicko* when I offered you *thirty pieces of silver,* so to speak. No, no. In fact, you were quite willing to betray your employer, now weren't you?"

"Man don't be trying to quote bible stuff to me! You ain't no kind of Christian!"

"I am who I am, *Judas.* And so are you."

"You gonna pay for this!"

"Speaking of *pay* – I expect you to give me my fifty-thousand dollars back, understood?"

"Don't count on it!"

"Oh, quite the contrary, *Judas.* Remember, I have your *collateral.*"

"Man you are one sick dude! You just better not hurt her!"

"C'mon now, *Judas.* Why worry? After all, she is in good hands – the hands of the *Good Samaritan*!"

CHAPTER THIRTY-TWO

ON FRIDAY MORNING GRANNY RAE called out repeatedly to her granddaughter. She'd tried waiting up for her last night, but soon fell asleep. "Diva! Diva!" Granny Rae's voice struggled to yell as loud as possible. There was no answer. She slowly inched her way through the den and into the living room where she peered out the window. Adiva's car wasn't in the driveway. It wasn't quite seven o'clock yet; surely her granddaughter hadn't left for work already. Especially without even saying goodbye.

Granny Rae's face grew drawn and pinched. She made her way back into the den and over to the sofa and sat down. She dialed Adiva's cell phone. There was no answer. Adiva usually kept her cell phone on at all times. Unsure of what to do next, Granny Rae decided to call Brother Blake.

Lorraine Brown was covering PPK's switchboard when Duke Priest arrived at the office. "Good morning, Lorraine," he greeted her cheerfully, a sunny feeling invigorating his soul. "Where's our lovely receptionist this morning?"

"Good morning, Mr. Priest," Lorraine greeted him. "Unfortunately, I haven't heard from Adiva yet."

"Really?" he attempted to look surprise. He glanced at his watch. "Oh dear - almost eight-thirty. I don't believe that Miss Roberts has ever been late before, has she?"

Lorraine shook her head. "No. In fact, Adiva is usually twenty minutes or more early every day. I'm going to try her at home in just a minute," Lorraine told him.

Duke began fiddling with his beard. "Mmmm. I tell you what - you seem to have your hands full with the switchboard - why don't I give Miss Roberts a call at home and see what's detaining her."

Lorraine felt a twinge of guilt. Adiva was her direct report. "Mr. Priest, you don't have to go through the trouble. I mean, I'll have a break in a few minutes and I'll . . . "

"No need to fret, dear. It's no trouble at all. It's just a phone call, right?"

Lorraine forced a sheepish smile. "Okay. Thanks. And let me know what you find out."

Duke gave her a wink. "Will do, my dear," he said as he walked briskly away heading toward his office. When he reached his office, he quickly closed the door behind him and exhaled. He realized that he was too close to success to have things unravel on him now. He sat down at his desk and waited for five minutes. Then he picked up his phone and punched the zero to get the front desk.

"Operator," Lorraine answered.

Duke cleared his throat. "Lorraine, I spoke with Miss Roberts a moment ago. The poor child sounds terribly ill – a virus of some kind, she believes."

"Oh no," Lorraine responded, disappointed and concerned.

"Yes, it is a shame. So naturally, I told her to remain at home. In fact, from the sound of her voice, we'd better plan on her being out perhaps two to three days."

"It's that serious?"

"One can never tell with a virus."

"Well, I guess I'll call some temp agencies and schedule a Temp for today through the middle of next week," Lorraine stated.

"Perhaps you'd better make it all of next week," Duke quickly added. "Just to be sure."

"Okay. I wonder if she needs anything – "

"No!" Duke shouted, before realizing that he'd done so. "I mean, I've already offered assistance and she says that everything is under control. I think she just wants to rest."

"That's understandable. Okay then. I'll do what needs to be done on this end."

"Yes, of course."

Brother Blake poured Granny Rae a hot cup of tea. "Drink this, Sister Roberts," he said, placing the burgundy cup and saucer in front of her. "This should help you to stay calm and relaxed."

"I'm just so worried 'bout my grandbaby," she told Brother Blake.

"I can understand how you must feel. But you know, the good Lord always keep watch over his children," he reminded her.

"But where she at!" Granny Rae screamed. "She ain't even come home last night! Sumthin' bad done happen to huh, I just knows it!"

"We're going to find her, Sister Roberts. Now, do you know the phone number at her job?" Brother Blake asked.

"Naw, I don't. 'Cause I calls Diva on her cell phone all the time."

"Okay, that's all right. What about the name of the place where she works?" he asked, figuring that he'd get the phone number from Information.

Granny Rae thought long and hard. "I knows she done told me the name, but I can't 'member," she bowed her head and began crying softly.

Brother Blake tried to comfort her some more. "Don't get yourself all upset, Sister Roberts. You've got to be strong now, okay?"

"What I's gon do if sumthin' happens to my grandbaby! She alls I got, Brother Blake! She alls I got . . . " her voice trailed off.

"This is a time when we need to call upon the Lord and trust in Him, Sister Roberts. You know he has never let his people down," Brother Blake admonished her.

Then the doorbell rang.

"Lawd Jesus! I hope that ain't the police with sum bad news 'bout my grandbaby!" Granny Rae wailed even louder.

Brother Blake went to answer the door. When he opened it, Soupa Mann stood on the other side. He introduced himself as Adiva's boyfriend. Brother Blake invited him inside.

Soupa Mann realized that Granny Rae would be worried about Adiva by now. He also knew that he had to find a way to convince her that Adiva was all right without divulging details because he didn't want her calling the police, which would place Adiva's life in greater danger.

Granny Rae was less than pleased when Soupa Mann emerged into the den. "Do you knows what happen to my grandbaby?" she immediately questioned him, her eyes narrowing with suspicion.

Soupa Mann braced himself.

"You do know sumthin' don't you Soupy!" she yelled at him. "What you done did with Diva, Soupy! What you done did!"

"Miss Roberts, please calm down. Adiva is all right," he told her, as Brother Blake also tried to calm Granny Rae.

"Let's hear what the young man has to say," Brother Blake appealed to Granny Rae.

Granny Rae remained silent for a moment to allow Soupa Mann to explain. However, her eyes regarded him with cold speculation as her lips curled with disgust.

Soupa Mann hoped that they would believe what he was about to tell them. He took a deep breath and then quickly exhaled. "Adiva met me for dinner yesterday evening," he began.

"Diva ain't say nuthin' to me 'bout no dinner with you, Soupy!" Granny Rae interrupted.

Brother Blake had to intervene again.

Soupa Mann went on to explain to them about Adiva's research project that she'd been working on for school. He told them that she'd come across some critical information. But, it was only available at the University of Georgia's library in Athens, Georgia. He further explained that Adiva decided to drive over to Athens last night. She spoke with a friend who said that she could stay with her while she was in Athens. Adiva had then planned to go to the UGA library today to gather the information she needed, Soupa Mann explained.

Of course, Granny Rae was aware that Adiva had a friend who lived in Athens, Georgia. And Soupa Mann was glad that he quickly remembered as well.

"How's come Diva didn't let me know 'bout this?" Granny Rae asked, her face tightly pinched.

"Well, she did tell me that she was gonna call you from the road. Something must have come up," Soupa Mann was running out of lies.

Brother Blake rested back against the sofa. His fingers were steepled and his face displayed a judicial expression. Soupa Mann doubted that he was buying his story.

"How's come she ain't call me this mo'ning?" Granny Rae continued to press.

Soupa Mann could only hunch his shoulders. "I'm sure she will, Miss Roberts." He then looked at his watch. "I gotta run," he told them. "But I'll try and reach Adiva myself this afternoon, Miss Roberts, and tell her to call you, okay?"

Granny Rae's eyes probed every inch of Soupa Mann's face. "If you says so," she finally uttered.

Soupa Mann quickly rose and hustled toward the front door. He thanked them for their time and he told Granny Rae that he'd be in touch.

He drove away from the house and then brought his Jeep to a stop once he was out of their sight. He grabbed his cell phone and dialed PPK's offices. Lorraine was still on the switchboard. When she answered, Soupa Mann said, "Hello - I want to talk to a *Princeton King*?"

"May I ask who's calling, please?"

"This is Soupa Mann."

"Oh, hey there!" Lorraine spoke, recognizing his name from her impromptu meeting with Adiva and Hannah yesterday. "So, is everything all right now?"

"Excuse me?"

"Well, yesterday Adiva was upset because she hadn't been able to reach you for a few days. But, I guess she finally did. Oh, and by the way, I'm sorry she's not feeling well?"

"Who is this?" Soupa Mann wanted to know.

"Oh, I'm Lorraine Brown. Adiva's supervisor."

"Uh huh. What do you mean *she's not feeling well?*"

Lorraine explained that one of the partners in the agency had called Adiva at home earlier this morning after she failed to show up for work. "Anyway, we found out that she's contracted some sort of virus – might be out for a few days."

The *Good Samaritan* had apparently covered his tracks. "Uh, did you actually speak to Adiva this morning?" Soupa Mann was curious of her response.

"Well, no. I didn't, but Mr. Priest offered to make the call."

"Mr. Priest?"

"One of the partners."

"I see. Well, I'm sure she's gonna be all right," he went along. "Now, may I speak to Princeton King – it's important?"

"Oh, of course. One moment." At the click of a button, Lorraine had transferred the call to Princeton's office.

"Princeton King," he answered.

"Hello. We've never met, but I'm Adiva's boyfriend," Soupa Mann began. "I need to see you right away, but not at your office."

"Whom am I speaking to?" Princeton wanted to know.

"I'm Soupa Mann—"

"Is this some kind of a joke?"

He figured he'd have to deal with this, so he spelled his name out slowly.

"*Soup* as in the can?" Princeton asked.

"You got it. And *Mann* with two *N's*."

"Soupa Mann - how creative," Princeton remarked. "Adiva never told me your name when she spoke of you."

"No problem. Anyway, Adiva is in trouble and . . . "

"What kind of trouble?" he interrupted.

"Hey, hear me out, okay? Now, I know she's been working with you on this whole CorpAir thing, and this is why we need to meet real quick - her life could be in danger."

Princeton's demeanor quickly took on a serious manner. Realizing that the phones were bugged, he said, "Don't say anything more on this line. Give me your number and I'll call you back in less than five minutes."

Soupa Mann gave him his cell phone number. "Okay. Give me five minutes!" He quickly punched zero on his phone. "Lorraine, where's Adiva?"

"She's home ill with a virus."

"You spoke with her?"

"No. Mr. Priest called her at home this morning."

"Duke? Why did he call her - doesn't she reports to you?"

"Yes, but he insisted."

"Okay, bye." Princeton hung the phone up and quickly grabbed his red blazer from behind his door and darted down the hallway. As he turned the corner he smashed into Duke Priest.

"Good grief, Princeton! Are you trying to run me over?"

"Sorry, Duke. I'm in a hurry."

"That I can see - you charged into me like a bat out of hell!"

"Again, I'm sorry," Princeton brushed himself off and Duke as well. "Hey, we need to talk later!" he yelled to Duke as he scrambled pass the receptionist's area.

"I'll be here!" Duke yelled back, though Princeton had already exited the offices.

Princeton encountered another near bodily collision as he leaped from the elevator as it stopped on the first floor - this time the victim was Hannah Prophet.

"My god, Princeton! Is it really that important that you have to knock me down?"

"I'm so sorry, Hannah. Something's come up - I gotta run!" He sprinted toward the exit.

"Does this have anything to do with Adiva?" Hannah yelled to him.

He skidded to a halt and ran back to her. "What do you know?"

"Well, first of all, I know what's going on between you two. And second of all, I told Adiva yesterday that I wouldn't say anything to my father until you guys got some solid proof, and . . . "

Princeton grabbed the girl's hand. "Smart move! Now come with me!" he told her, ushering her toward the building's exit.

"Where are we going?" she asked, struggling to keep pace with him.

"Just come along – we'll chat later!"

CHAPTER THIRTY-THREE

PRINCETON HAD DRIVEN TO THE Starbucks down the street from PPK's office building. He parked his car in the parking lot as he called Soupa Mann.

Soupa Mann explained to him how he got involved in the CorpAir matter. He shared with Princeton how he met the gentleman, who referred to himself as the *Good Samaritan.* He went on to explain the events of last Friday, both at CorpAir and at his apartment. Then he told Princeton what happened while he was speaking with Adiva on the phone yesterday evening.

"So, you're saying that when you were speaking with her last, you'd just given her a description of the gentleman who you've been meeting with?" Princeton asked, still trying to sort things out.

"Yeah," Soupa Mann answered. "She'd said something like she knew all along it was the owner of the agency," Soupa Mann continued. "But I think it was when I referred to his bald head that really threw her."

"PPK's owner – at least majority owner – doesn't have a bald head," Princeton replied. "Tell you what – give me a full description of the guy you've been meeting with about CorpAir," he instructed Soupa Mann.

Soupa Mann repeated the same description that he'd given to Adiva yesterday.

Princeton's eyes widened with amazement. "Well, now I can see why she would have been shocked," he remarked. "You've just described the other partner in the agency - Duke Priest."

"Priest?" Soupa Mann repeated. "Yeah, that's the name your receptionist gave me this morning when she told me who called Adiva at home to find out she was sick."

"Yes, she told me that as well. Listen, it appears that Adiva is probably being held at Duke Priest's home . . ."

"Where he live at!" Soupa Mann demanded. "I'm going over there!"

"Whoa, not so fast," Princeton told him. "I know that Duke is still at the office, so we need to make sure that he stays there."

Soupa Mann agreed. "So what we gon do?"

Princeton thought for a moment. He was having a difficult time believing that Duke Priest was in fact the one behind PPK's client mishaps. Why would Duke even care if the agency lost a client when he mostly talked about leaving the agency anyway? Princeton even recalled Duke telling him last month that he'd probably give up his fifteen-percent share to Harvard, and of course, Princeton had gotten him to agree to sell him the shares first. He surmised that Duke couldn't possibly be in his right mind. Apparently, his weekly sessions with the psychiatrist were not helping him much.

"Can you meet me here at the Starbucks on Peachtree Street?" Princeton asked Soupa Mann.

Soupa Mann said that he could.

"Good. We've got less than two hours to find Adiva and stop that CorpAir plane from taking off."

◈◈◈◈◈◈◈

After Soupa Mann met Princeton and Hannah at the Starbucks, it was decided that he and Hannah would go and check out Duke Priest's home. It was the most logical place that Duke had probably taken Adiva last night. Princeton decided to head back to the office to see if he could perhaps appeal to Duke's rational side.

The Jeep Cherokee turned quickly into the driveway of Duke Priest's north suburban home. Soupa Mann and Hannah leaped from the vehicle and scampered toward the rear of the house. They knew that they would more than likely have to shatter a window or something, so the back of the house would provide them with more privacy, even though the house sat far away from the street and was shielded by trees on both sides.

They'd decided not to call in the police as yet. Princeton did say, however, that if Soupa Mann and Hannah had not heard from him by ten thirty, they were to first call the FAA and then CorpAir about the impending explosion aboard flight 2900.

Soupa Mann wasted no time in using a large rock that he'd retrieved from Duke's flower garden to smash in the window on the back door, just above the doorknob. They expected to hear an alarm go off but one didn't. He reached inside the broken window and unlocked the door. Once inside, they immediately ran throughout the house shouting Adiva's name.

"She's probably bound and gagged," Soupa Mann said. "Let's find the basement!"

They found a door just off the foyer that led downstairs to the basement. They flipped on the light switch and raced down the steps. The basement had been neatly finished and carpeted. They could hear moaning from the other side of the basement. Soupa Mann and Hannah sprinted over and found a storage closet.

"She's in here!" Soupa Mann shouted, trying to open the storage closet's door. The door was locked. The moans grew louder. "We need to find something to pry this door open!" he yelled at Hannah.

Hannah began a frantic search.

"Hold on Adiva! I'm coming!" he shouted through the door.

Hannah grew nervous, as she could find nothing to pry the door open. "I don't see anything!" she screamed, nearly panicking.

Soupa Mann noticed a fire extinguisher hanging on the wall. He grabbed it and began pounding it against the door until the door cracked. Eventually a hole was made into the door that was large enough for him to reach his arm inside and turn the doorknob.

Adiva was found lying sideways on the floor. Her mouth had been covered with duct tape and her hands and feet were tied with extension cords. Soupa Mann and Hannah rushed over to her and began untying the cords. Then Soupa Mann gently peeled the duct tape from her mouth.

Once free, Adiva threw her arms around Soupa Mann. "Thank God!" she cried. Then she embraced Hannah and immediately told her how sorry she was for suspecting her father.

Soupa Mann filled Adiva in. He told her that Princeton wanted an opportunity to try and reason with Duke Priest.

"But we're running out of time!" she told him.

Soupa Mann looked at his watch. It was 10:05. "I know. C'mon, let's make our way out to the airport – we can call the authorities from the car!"

Princeton King knew that he had no time to spare. He marched down to Duke Priest's office.

Duke was perusing some papers. He didn't notice Princeton come in. Princeton shut the door behind him.

"It's over, Duke," he said, taking a seat in one of the chairs that were in front of Duke's desk.

Duke looked up, allowing his pen to fall to his desk pad. "Good grief, Princeton. First you try and run me over and now you're sneaking up on me!"

"I know the deal, Duke. And it's over."

Duke stared at him like the proverbial cat that had eaten the canary. "What on earth are you talking about?" he asked dubiously.

"Can the charade, Duke. Adiva and I figured it all out. Why? How could you do such things?"

Duke, unwilling to neither admit nor face defeat, removed his glasses from his face and stuck one end of the frame's tip into his mouth. "I don't expect you to understand," he began, staring past Princeton.

"Try me," Princeton told him.

Duke displayed a shameless grin. "This agency became my life, Princeton. It represented my very essence."

Princeton couldn't believe what he was hearing. He'd expected Harvard Prophet to utter such words, but not Duke. "But you told me many times how much you hated this place," Princeton reminded him.

"I know. Call it bittersweet. But I realized that without it, I didn't exist."

"So basically, you felt that if we lost certain clients, the agency itself would be in jeopardy?"

"Certainly. Princeton, we operate with five clients - five profitable clients, mind you. And the loss of even one would have easily sent us into a downward spiral."

"But why did you feel the need to take it upon yourself to *save* the agency, Duke? Harvard had more to lose than you or I! And besides, we could have secured other clients!"

"Perhaps. But it wouldn't have been the same. You see, once PPK made its mark as having never lost a client, I simply could not sit back and allow that mark to become tarnished."

"Duke, do you realize how many people have been killed by your actions?"

Duke replaced his horn-rimmed glasses and stared coldly at Princeton. "Casualties of war, my friend."

Princeton shook his head in disbelief. "I want you to pick up that phone and call CorpAir and tell them about flight 2900," he ordered Duke, looking at his watch.

Duke's eyes narrowed with contempt. "CorpAir - good ol' CorpAir. Our bread and butter for so many years. But, you know what, Princeton? The client isn't always right after all."

Princeton just glared at him.

"No, no. The client wants us to believe that they're always right, but they're not!" he became adamant. "We know what's right for them, don't we!"

Princeton chose not to respond.

"Of course we do. They were not going to choose us again, Princeton. CorpAir had no intentions of selecting PPK. They were going to seal our fate by yanking their precious account. A bit unfair, wouldn't you say, Princeton? Our future, yours and everyone else's, all resting in the hands of one client!"

"Make the call, Duke!" Princeton grew impatient.

Duke laughed to himself. "Guess who else is not without fault, Princeton?" he paused a moment. "Ah, good ol' Harvey boy!"

"Harvard didn't create these mishaps, Duke. You did, along with whomever you may have hired to help you."

"Right you are, Princeton. But, I guarantee you that if I hadn't done so, Harvey boy would have!"

"You don't know that for sure."

"Oh, but I do! Any man who would stoop so low as to bug his own employees, not to mention his partners, would do just about anything!"

"So, you knew that the offices were bugged and being videotaped?"

"Most definitely!" Duke answered. He then turned his face toward a corner of the ceiling and waved to the hidden camera. "Hello, Harvey!" he mocked. "You tried to screw me over and all of these years I've been saving your agency! You owe me Harvey! You owe me big!" he yelled at the camera, shaking his fist defiantly.

"Screw you how?" Princeton picked up on his statement.

"Well, little did you know Princeton, but the old man found out that I was seeing a shrink and so he decided to pay the good doctor a large sum of money for him to try and convince me - his patient - that I needed to rid myself of the agency! Sell my shares to him of all people!"

Princeton was totally shocked by the revelation. Apparently Harvard's hands were not so clean after all. "How did you find this out?" Princeton was curious.

"The good doctor told me himself! The man was so guilt ridden that he shut his practice down and left the state! But you know what? He and I had the last laugh!" Duke's face glistened with pleasure for a moment. "Yes, indeed. We had the last laugh!"

"Duke, don't hurt any more innocent people," Princeton pleaded. "This is where it all ends. Make the call, please?"

"Well, Princeton. You are right about one thing; *this* is where it all ends." Duke reached down and opened the bottom drawer on his desk and slowly removed a small black pistol. As he positioned the pistol to the right side of his temple, Princeton's face became masked with horror. But before Princeton could lunge across the desk to prevent his cohort from doing the unthinkable, Duke squeezed the trigger. The gun fell quickly to the floor and Duke Priest slumped over his desk, blood pouring from the side of his head.

CHAPTER THIRTY-FOUR

IT WAS 10:50 WHEN SOUPA MANN'S JEEP Cherokee exited off Interstate-85 South on the ramp leading to the airport. Adiva had tried to reach an FAA official on Soupa Mann's cell phone, but the connection went dead while she was on hold.

"Try and get a connection now," Hannah suggested from the backseat.

Adiva pressed the power button on the cell phone. "Still dead," she reported. "It looks like it's up to us to stop that plane from taking off."

"And how you think we gon do that?" Soupa Mann asked, as he sped around a curve.

"We've got to do something, Soupa Mann," Adiva told him.

Hannah moved to the center of the backseat in an effort to feel more involved in the discussions. "We can always go directly to CorpAir's offices and have them stop the plane," she offered.

She means well, Adiva thought to herself. "Trust me, Hannah. We won't have time for all that. I mean, the plane is scheduled to take off at eleven o'five – everyone is probably already on the plane by now. Anyway, who would we contact at CorpAir?

I'm sure everybody who is *somebody* is sure to be on the flight."

"Adiva's right," Soupa Mann piped in. "We're almost out of time as it is. Let's just hope that flight 2900 is like most flights!" he said.

"What do you mean?" Hannah asked him.

"That they're late!"

The trio made it to the airport with only five minutes before flight 2900 would be taking off. Each of them had become frantic. "Where in the heck am I supposed to go now?" Soupa Mann questioned anyone who'd answer.

"We need to try and find the plane!" Adiva yelled at him.

"What!"

"That's the only chance we have left! There's no time to do anything else!"

"Dahling, what are you suggesting?" Hannah asked, nervously.

"What I'm *telling* you, not *suggesting,* is that the only way we're going to stop that plane from taking off is to drive this Jeep in front of it!"

"Baby, you must be out your mind!" Soupa Mann laughed.

"I think she's serious," Hannah interjected.

"First off, how in the heck do we find the plane? And then if we find it, what makes you think we gon be able to drive this little Jeep across the runway in front of it? I mean do you realize how fast airport security will have our butts surrounded?"

"Soupa Mann, that's a chance we'll just have to take!" Adiva said angrily. "I say we take our chances and put the pedal to the metal and find the darn plane! If we do nothing more than create a chaotic scene, then hopefully it will be enough for the airport to shut down."

"I hope you right," Soupa Mann responded.

"Guys, it doesn't matter whether the plane takes off or not - either way the bomb is set to go off at eleven-twenty," Hannah reminded them. "So, unless we can stop it, CorpAir flight 2900 will either explode in the air or on the runway."

Neither Adiva nor Soupa Mann responded. But they knew Hannah was exactly right. Soupa Mann accelerated the speed of the Jeep. He decided to take a wild guess as to which runway the plane would be taking off from. The blue and white aircraft wouldn't be difficult to spot. However, getting the Jeep to maneuver across the runways while dodging other aircraft at the same time was going to be the challenge.

◈◈◈◈◈◈◈

"Ladies' and gentlemen . . . " the pilot's dry voice oozed from the intercom. " . . . we've just been informed by the control tower that an unusual event is unfolding. Apparently, a passenger vehicle has been spotted racing across the runways. The authorities are in pursuit of the vehicle as we speak. Unfortunately, this will delay our scheduled departure momentarily. Your patience is greatly appreciated."

Immediately, groans erupted throughout the cabin. Then one of the passengers onboard shouted as he pointed out his window. "There it is! I see it! It's heading our way!"

Everyone scrambled to a window on the left side of the plane to try and catch a glimpse of the *unfolding event*. The Jeep Cherokee certainly appeared to be heading toward the CorpAir jet, followed by a plethora of police cars and other emergency vehicles.

Adiva had been able to get the cell phone working again as Soupa Mann sped across the runways. She telephoned airport officials and told them that a bomb had been planted aboard CorpAir flight 2900 and that they were, at this very moment, driving across the runway in a burgundy Jeep, attempting to stop the airplane from taking off.

As she peered through the rear window of the Jeep, she hoped that the legion of police cars and fire trucks, all with sirens blaring, that were approaching behind them were fully aware of the situation. She did not think that she could withstand having an array of guns being pointed at her.

The Jeep drew near to the CorpAir plane. Suddenly the doors of the plane flew open and the emergency chutes were inflated. A slew of passengers began sliding down the chutes and running across the open runway. Soupa Mann, Adiva and Hannah cheered and clapped their hands.

Soon, police cars and other emergency vehicles had surrounded the plane. The remaining passengers and crew were quickly rushed across the runway as the time ticked to 11:17. It was determined that there wasn't ample time to send a bomb squad aboard the plane to locate and diffuse the device, so the immediate area was hastily evacuated.

Soupa Mann had also driven the Jeep a safe distance from the plane. The three of them exited the Jeep and stood among the crowd.

It was now sixty-seconds before the bomb would detonate.

Then it happened. A tremendous explosion erupted, sending the crowd ducking and some falling to the ground. When they looked back toward the airplane they could see nothing but a massive fireball and scattered debris. Fire trucks quickly converged toward the area. The passengers who'd been sitting on the airplane just moments ago were stunned, yet very thankful. Some wept openly as they considered what might have been.

Soupa Mann, Adiva and Hannah embraced one another. Adiva offered a silent prayer of thanksgiving. Hannah couldn't keep from crying. She wrestled with trying to understand how anyone could even contemplate destruction of such massive proportion.

Officials began to usher them all away from the area and onto scores of blue buses that had arrived to take them back to the airport terminal.

EPILOGUE

PROPHET, PRIEST & KING HAD BECOME A phenomenon. The once infallible ad agency could not withstand the aggression in the aftermath of the CorpAir catastrophe. PPK had become a victim of its own unparalleled success. The agency's clients had come to symbolize the epitome of client relationship management. And one man had sought to keep the agency's dream alive and flourishing.

Although Duke Priest had only owned fifteen-percent of the once highly regarded agency, he'd given one hundred percent of his all to it. It ultimately cost him his marriage, his sanity and his life. He died alone and unfulfilled.

Six months later, Harvard Prophet sold PPK to his nemesis, Young & Lucas out of New York. Y&L had also won the CorpAir account - without even going through the final presentations stage.

Harvard decided to leave the ad agency business altogether, choosing instead to spend more quality time with his daughter, who decided not to return to London. It would be her *D-Day* - daughter day - for as long as she wanted.

Seymour Boudreau relinquished his obsession with Harvard. He accepted a similar position with the

Young & Lucas agency. He'd developed a sudden interest in Goodwin Young.

Princeton King reconciled with his wife and kids. However, it was conditioned on the fact that he move back to Chicago, which he did; and that he enter into rehabilitation, which he also did. He also left the agency business and decided to teach at the University of Illinois.

Soupa Mann had to face charges for his role in allowing the bomb to be planted aboard CorpAir. Because he had no prior criminal record, he was fined heavily and received a suspended sentence. He'd also retained the money that Duke Priest had given him, which he'd socked away in the bank, so he was able to have his demo tape professionally made.

Adiva Roberts decided to write about advertising rather than create it. She joined the Atlanta office of *Advertising Age* magazine as a reporter. The following Valentine's Day, she and Soupa Mann became engaged. She was deeply hurt that her grandmother would never see the blessed event - Granny Rae had died on Christmas Eve.

◈◈◈◈◈◈◈

One spring evening, Adiva was having dinner with Hannah at the Buckhead Fish Market. Hannah had been telling her that Radford Albright was now living in the U.S. She was debating whether or not she should contact him. Although she'd admitted that the two of them did have a semi-serious relationship while at the University in London.

Adiva advised her, "Girl, you better make your attack while the skillet is burning!"

Hannah looked confused. Then she promptly replied, "Dahling, you do mean to say *strike while the iron is hot*!"

They both roared with laughter.

What A Difference A Shade Makes

From the crayons in a box
So many colors are used to create
Pictures of green grass, blue moons
Or a purple haze across a lake

If all the colors were but one
Our eyes might just as well be blind
For we need more than pink, gray and brown
If we are ever to expand the creative mind

It is in the combining of the many colors
That allow us to accomplish so much
There is no harm in mixing yellow and orange
If two beautiful colors need to touch

So let us open wide our eyes
To absorb, understand and appreciate
Whether red, black or white
What a difference a shade makes

– Cornell Graham